iece of Me

daughter of ... ess

Catherine Schiffer

Energy4PR
Publishers
"your story;
their hope"

This publication is designed to provide authoritative information with regard to the subject matter covered. It is sold as
a self-help and personal improvement resource with the understanding that the author and publisher are not engaged in
rendering professional advice. If advice or expert assistance is
needed including but not limited to financial, physical, mental or
emotional, the services of a competent and licensed professional
should be sought.

The author and publication team have given every effort to credit
quotes and thoughts that aren't original with the author. The
personal accounts in this publication are written as the author
remembers them.

Book Cover Photo Ceredit: Stevie Dee Photography
Book Cover & Interior Design by Energy4PR Publishers.

Paperback ISBN: 978-1-64871-633-1
Digital ISBN: 978-1-64871-600-3
Pieces of Me: A Daughter of Mental Illness

Connect @ catherineschiffer.com

Table of Contents

"Unwanted and insecure, at the age of 12 my life trials began, always making sure I went on the most difficult path: abused, alcohol, drugs, etc. It took many years to find my true worth. Now at 53, I'm learning each day life is worth living and I am worth it. I have a long road, but I will never give up. Living with a depressed, alcoholic mother takes you into a downward spiral: never good enough, never wanted and highly insecure! I was always running. Abused physically and mentally, I turned to drugs and alcohol as a way out. I wish I knew; I wish I believed I was worth it! Catherine brought out so many memories and took me back to the start. My therapist recently told me to write it all down from my first memory to now. I am going to do just that. I love you, and I am so proud of you!"

- Jamie Humphreys, Friend

"Catherine Schiffer is a beacon of hope! Her resilience is nothing short of inspiring. This book and her story are proof of her courageous heart. It is also proof of how the love of God can and does transform lives. The message and words of this book will serve to help heal the hearts of those who have experienced the pain of abuse and violence. Catherine has walked through trials and has overcome obstacles that cannot be imagined. She is a valiant beautiful force and a light in this world. I would recommend this book to anyone, whether they have experienced abuse or not; the level of faith and love that pours out of Catherine's heart through these pages needs to be shared!"

**- Michelle Schaffer, Author of *Redefined* &
"Girl Power Alliance" Podcast Host**

"Many live in denial about their past, suffer in the present and miss the future God has planned for them. With courgageous strokes of her pen, Catherine allows you to open up about your past realizing only the enemy wins when our mind is locked in the prison of trauma behind the bars of shame & guilt. *Pieces of Me* will inspire anyone who has experienced trauma to look at seemingly broken pieces as a beautiful mosaic in the hands of our Father!"

- Tim Hooper, Speaker & Author of *GotEnergy?*

"I can't stop thinking about Catherine Schiffer's book, *Pieces of Me*. First, for the obvious reasons ... that no one should have to endure a childhood of suffering in the magnitude she did. I found myself in tears as I pictured that sweet little girl who faced battle and survival. Second, and this is the most important ... she not only survived, she went on to become one of the most successful people in her field and a powerful influence in raising awareness and creating a movement to stop the heartbreaking tragedy of child abuse and addiction. Her book made me look back on my own childhood as a blessing, and to not take it for granted. It also made me want to honor my privileged childhood by helping others who didn't have it so safe. It made me ask the questions, what can I do to change this for other children? How can I help? Schiffer writes her book so poignantly, and you can feel the child and hear her child's voice as she details what she suffered and how she survived. She writes openly and honestly about the struggle she has had with addiction, and the triumphant times that show just how strong and resilient she really is. I am sure this book will stay with me for a long time ... not the tragedy, but the triumph of the author, who she's become, and the lives she will change because she had the courage to speak out."

- Sandy Peckinpah, Award-Winning Author of *How to Survive the Worst that Can Happen*

Dedication

This book is dedicated to the millions of men and women, boys and girls who have had the unfortunate experience of physical, sexual, spiritual or emotional abuse as part of their story.

To those who feel thrown away and abandoned by the ones entrusted to keep them safe.

To the people lost in addiction due to the pain of the past.

To my children and all the children who suffer in the crossfire of our addiction.

To those strong and valiant warriors who stood up in the face of evil and addiction and said, "No More"!

I dedicate this book to anyone who has had to relearn life.

I commend you for taking the hard route of recovery and change.

We are the winners!

I pray you are blessed by God's story of justification and restoration, in His name,

Amen

Foreword

I love the title of Catherine Schiffer's book - *Pieces of Me*. It is a very accurate depiction of the type of journey people choose to enter into when they are ready to find the healing and freedom that Jesus provides. It is a difficult, painful and scary road that many people choose to avoid. It doesn't always make sense and it is difficult to navigate when you start with just "pieces".

That is what makes Catherine's book so special. She describes her pilgrimage from the eyes of her as a child and as an adult. She tells her story weaving the past and the present together to give the reader an up close and personal understanding of the pain, terror and trauma that was inflicted upon her as she was growing up. Sadly her story is all too familiar to so many.

As a Marriage and Family therapist, I have had the great privilege and honor of walking with many folks down their own path of tragedy to triumph. As Catherine describes in this book, it wasn't just the physical, sexual and emotional abuse that she was healing from ... it was also the lies that she came to believe about herself. Those lies, as she describes, became her "truth". She knew nothing else. This, as with so many others, was all she knew.

The enemy of our souls, Satan, wants nothing more than to steal, kill and destroy (John 10:10). He does this, in no small part, by implanting lies in a child's heart and mind. When adults use their power to inflict harm and trauma upon a child, the seeds of lies are planted. These lies take the form of "I don't matter", "I am not worth loving", "there is something horribly wrong with me" just to name a few. These lies impact everything we think, feel, say and do. We will do most anything to alleviate the pain. As this book describes, we will even turn to self-destructive means to temporarily ease the pain.

Catherine explains this process of self-destruction in simple and yet profound ways. She takes the reader into her world piece by piece and all along the way explains that it was her Heavenly Father who helped her begin and continue her journey to healing and wholeness by the power of His love, grace and truth.

My hope and prayer as you read this book is if you find yourself in the same places as Catherine, that the seeds of hope would be planted in your heart and mind that you too can experience the same healing and freedom as she has. God has an amazing way of working through our painful stories to help bring help, hope and healing to others. I know this is Catherine's hope and prayer also.

Kathy Moratto LMFT

Prologue

My mind is a constant firestorm of words, phrases and sayings as my thoughts race and race day after day. Sometimes the same things loop through my mind over and over, and other times it's constantly changing.

I have found that writing, putting it down on paper is the best way to get it out and move onto the next thing in my mind. I have so much to say and not sure the direction or format in which to put it.

As I set out on this arduous task of telling my story I have to look at my motives. Is it to hurt someone? Is it to get back the dignity that was stripped away? Am I trying to recover the respect and honor for all the years of therapy, wasted time, loss of quality of life and medicating with drugs? Or, is it truly to show hope and point people toward a God who is bigger than any circumstance, situation, or pain that we might be carrying.

Honestly?

Through much introspection, I can clearly say at first my main motivation was to tell the world "Look what they did to me!" But by the time I finished this book, my motivation had changed. Today I want to tell the world, " Look what God has done for me!"

This book has changed me. It took me three years to write. There were months at a time I couldn't pick it up. I dealt with anger, resentment and grief, the grief of innocence lost. The grief of so many years wasted, running and running. Running from pain, running from people, but most of all running from God.

I want this book to inspire you and motivate you, but most of all show you that there is an answer to our pain and struggle. I want to share how I discovered hope for those of us who have been victimized and deprived of love and acceptance. Deprived of a family that was supposed to keep us safe but instead became our living nightmares.

I want this book to minister to your bondage by showing you that medicating with drugs, alcohol, sex, food, exercise, work, etc. is not the answer either. Oh sure it works, until it doesn't, and then we are left with the original pain compiled by more wreckage that we have created by our choices. I don't blame myself, we don't know what we don't know!

Most of all, I want to share with you the God who met me right where I was deep in the pit. He reached down and said, "Grab on little one and I will pull you out. Just trust me and I will make all things new."

Revelation 21:5 "Behold I make everything new."

As many survivors know the first thing we lose is our voice, we are taught to keep secrets and not speak truth. If we do speak the truth we are called liars and troublemakers. This is magnified if there is an enabler in the home protecting the predator. There is no one on our side. We are all alone with our dark secrets, hiding from the world.

This book is my message to the brokenhearted, the downtrodden, the throwaways, to the many men and women who live in constant defeat, in a battle with life. Those who open their eyes each morning and are angry they are still alive; who ask God what is the purpose? Why did you create me?

I often asked, What kind of God are you that you would allow such horrible acts to be perpetrated on an innocent child and then to reach adulthood with no coping skills, relational skills or even some of us the ability to function as normal adults? Are we truly to be held accountable for our actions at this point?

Of course, we are medicating, running, looking for love from person-to-person, lying and stealing from others. We were taught that this was the way to survive. We have no identity, no purpose.

This was me, My story will tell of an innocence lost and a child betrayed by her very own blood. Then, you will hear of a young adult who was doing exactly what one would expect from a victim of violent crimes, who then would be blamed and become the black sheep because of her choices.

You will hear of more abuse by the men she chose. You will hear of years of drug use, sexual sickness, abuse by her put onto the ones she loved the most, and finally jails and institutions.

But then, you will hear of an awakening, a light, a change that is a slow regeneration and a compelling truth. A new life coming from the ashes and exploding into the atmosphere, a life that will turn heads, bring restoration and healing to many, and ultimately a woman who has purpose.

More than anything else, you will hear of a God who loves us, a God who cried when I cried, a God who fights for us and renders us complete and brand new. You will learn about Jesus who will stand before us and declare us innocent to the Father; who will wash away all the crimson stains, the shame, the anger, bitterness and hopelessness!

A God who will restore relationships and families, a God who will wash away years of suffering and turn them into something beautiful. *A God who will use the pain and suffering to bring healing by using the very thing the enemy wanted to destroy her with to bring hope to so many.*

Are you ready to lay down the weapons, to turn vengeance over to a very just God, to stop hiding from the pain in a person, place, or thing? Are you ready to start a journey of discovering, you? Then join me on my own journey of discovery laid out in these pages.

This book is different than most books as each chapter tells a new story of tragedy and triumph, this story is told in pieces, which ultimately make up, *All the Pieces of Me!*

*"I want you to hear
of a God who fights
for us and renders us
complete and
brand new."*

The Dawn of Remembrance

Chapter 1

"Sometimes memories sneak out of my eyes and roll down my cheeks" - Unknown

I suddenly woke up to the feeling of my covers being pulled down. It felt cold, but the kind of cold that rose up from the inside; frozen with fear.

I lay as still as possible pretending to be asleep. I thought maybe if I couldn't be woken up, it would stop.

He lifts me from my warm bed. I peeked across the room at the little blonde baby girl, my sister, nestled into her soft, warm blankets. She was sleeping safely. I felt jealous and wished I was her but glad she wasn't me.

That doesn't mean she didn't suffer the same abuse I did, but this is my story.

I don't know why I didn't scream, I don't know why I didn't fight. Had it happened before?

I continued to fake sleep as he carried me into another room. I opened my eyes ever so slightly, I could see brown walls all around, and a dim light drifting in from the hallway. The room had a musty, pungent smell. I felt sickened by it, and knowing... how did I know? I lay still but shivering inside from the cold... and the fear.

I felt myself lowered onto cushions and there was a wood banister at the end of the couch.

Through the banister I could see my mother sleeping; she lay across her bed with no clothes on, I remember this so vividly. I wanted to scream out, I wanted to ask her for help, but the words stuck in my throat. It was as if I knew at some visceral level that it wouldn't even matter.

"Why would someone do this? Please stop! Please stop!"

I felt cold hands unbutton the bottom of my nightgown, and it was slowly pushed up towards my chest. It seemed so familiar. I wasn't quite sure what was about to happen, but it was as though I knew exactly what to do. Lie still.

It was a horrible feeling, I didn't like it! I wanted to cry. But I didn't. Why would someone do this?

Please stop! Please stop! Please stop! These are the words that screamed in my head, but I knew what to do. Lie still.

I began to fade out to a happier place. I saw myself bouncing across the street to our neighbor's house, Mr. Blankenship.

My hair is in blonde pigtails, and I'm wearing a sundress, as it is the middle of summer in Louisiana. I can smell the dirt. I can hear the rustle of leaves under my little white sandals and the sound of the wind blowing through the trees.

It's peaceful there, and Mr. Blankenship will have gum for me. I get closer to my friend's home and see him sitting on the front porch. I skip over delightfully with my rosy pink cheeks and ask him ever so kindly for a stick of gum. He is always such a kind man; he never raises his voice. He never touches me in places that make me feel uncomfortable. I never want to leave his front porch. I felt so safe there.

"Suddenly, my mind brings me back into this uncomfortable, scary place!"

We sit on his porch for a very long time as I rattle on with my questions as every little child does.

The Dawn of Remembrance

"Why is the sky blue? Where do clouds come from? Why does it rain? How do trees get so big?" and on and on I went.

I would notice him chuckle at some of my questions, and so I would go on as I enjoyed his patience and kindness.

The gum rolls around in my mouth as I drink in the deliciousness of it, I loved gum. I loved the bubbles I could blow, the popping that would sometimes occur and of course the sweetness it always offered.

I sat back and closed my eyes as I enjoyed this tasty treat.

Suddenly, my mind brings me back into this uncomfortable, scary place.

My panties are being tugged back up, and my nightgown is pulled down. I am lifted off the couch and taken back to my bedroom, and I still pretend to be asleep.

I was three years old and this is the dawn of remembrance ... the very first memory I have of waking up to my life.

"I know the plans I have for you - they are for good and not evil!"

Your Notes

What painful memories haunt you?
Perhaps you've buried them deep
down; but, by writing them here, you
agree with me to allow the light of
God's truth to free you:

_____

_____

_____

_____

_____

_____

_____

_____

_____

_____

_____

_____

_____

_____

_____

_____

_____

Angels In Earthly Form

Chapter 2

"Sometimes people come into your life for a moment, a day, or a lifetime. It matters not the time you spend with them but how they impact your life in that time."
- Unknown

*T*oday is beautiful. I love living in Southern California where the sky is a deep blue and the temperature is a perfect 82 degrees, especially while I'm sitting by the pool watching my grandkids swim. So carefree, so trusting.

I look at them and feel a huge responsibility to be a light in their lives. I want to be a safe haven for them, now and as they grow up. I have a responsibility on my heart to teach them how to protect themselves and other survival skills that will help them become good human beings. But more importantly, I want them to know they are loved. Loved by me, their parents and a Heavenly Father.

These babies are my gift, my second chance at getting it right!

As mothers, we sometimes feel as though we fail, even when we think we're doing it the "right way." I have children I've raised when I was using drugs, and a child I raised when I was sober. They all have struggles, so just start saving for therapy now! (LOL)

I recently had the privilege to sit with a group of women for a book study. We all shared our struggles. One of the beautiful women shared how perfect her life was when she was growing up. She felt she was over-protected, and when it came time to face the real world, she was defenseless and unprepared for real life. This story helped me to put into perspective that we all are a little broken in our own way no matter our upbringing.

I am now a mother to grown daughters who have their own children. I feel a great desire to partner with my kids and give them strength when they feel weak. I want to be able to offer advice when my children feel lost, and spend time with their babies, giving their parents the opportunity for rest and reconnection with their lives their friends and their spouses.

"We are a tribe, and it does take a village."

We are a tribe, and it does take a village!

So how could it be that some mothers don't feel the desire to protect their young?

What could compel a mother to not only perpetuate her own emotional and physical abuse, but to allow a man to sexually assault her child and turn her back on the cries for help?

When I was just three years old my mother brought a man into our home who would become my attacker for the next eleven years. She was his enabler and partner in the abuse. The woman whom I loved so much was to become the enemy of my life.

Her family of origin is very large, and she had a very strict Christian upbringing. She was one of seven daughters and the fourth born girl. She met my dad at a young age and found herself pregnant at fifteen. She told me that the pregnancy was an embarrassment to the family, and I was not wanted. In fact, I was taken straight from the hospital to a foster home where I spent the first six months of my life.

"He became my attacker for the next eleven years."

I was told by my mom that my grandparents finally relented to her pleas to marry my father and soon after I was brought home from the foster family.

So, there I was, a six month-old baby torn from the only mother she knew and given to a strange man and woman. Not the happy beginning for any child and not the happy beginning I am sure my mom expected either.

My dad was just nineteen when I was born. He never spoke of his feelings for my mom or much about their relationship as I grew up. I learned my dad was arrested when I was two years old for selling narcotics to an undercover police officer and incarcerated until I was five.

I remember going to the jail to visit him. There was a large picnic area with tables, and I remember those being happy visits, filled with lots of hugs and kisses from him; something I never recall experiencing with my mother.

While my dad was in jail my mother went to work at a fast food eatery to make ends meet. Across the street from where she worked in Monrovia, California there was a real estate brokerage. The man who would become my stepdad owned the brokerage and met my mother while having lunch at her work. They began dating. She was nineteen and he was forty-five.

"There I was, a six-month-old baby, torn from the only mother I knew."

One day, this man's wife visited my mother's work. She warned my mother they were in the process of divorce because he had sexually assaulted both of his daughters. Since my mother had two young girls, the wife felt compelled to warn her. She threatened to prosecute him unless he moved out of California (I learned this information in 2018 while researching this book).

I wish I could say that my mother was appalled and disgusted. I wish I could say she immediately ended any kind of relationship with this man, but alas, that was not to be the case.

Within weeks, He was her new boyfriend.

Of course, I do not remember the exact time the abuse began, but it did, just as the former wife had predicted. And perhaps her threats of criminal action were real because my mother and her boyfriend moved out of California, leaving my sister and me behind. I don't know the details of her running off, I just remember her being gone and we were then shuffled back and forth

"I remember her being gone; we were then shuffled back and forth."

between my Nanny, my Auntie Maude, and my Grandma Robbins for the next several years, eventually living with my Dad when he was released from prison.

My Nanny

The first person I remember telling was my Nanny. She wasn't a childcare provider as "Nanny" would mean, but she was my mother's aunt. Her name was Susan, but we all called her Nanny. I remember these years as happy and filled with fun and adventure. I wasn't being touched in areas that made me feel scared. I felt safe.

Nanny loved me, and she often let me cuddle with her on her lap. She'd tuck me into bed at night and tell wonderful stories of a man named Jesus. This was not just any man, but this was the God man.

Nanny had a delightful and comforting English accent. She smelled of roses and Ben-Gay cream all at the same time. She was a large woman, but to me she was soft and cuddly, and I loved listening to her recount story after story of how Jesus loved me and wanted me to love Him.

I heard of Noah, a boat, and a great rainstorm that carried off the boat to a new land. She explained how his family was saved and protected. She recounted how Moses set all the slaves free from being hurt every day. I also heard about a boy named Joseph who had a beautiful coat that made his brothers jealous. They threw him into a hole, yet Joseph was rescued by God to go to a new land and became a ruler! I loved hearing these stories, Jesus seemed so kind and safe, and I wanted Him to protect me from the bad people in my life.

> *"She'd tell wonderful stories of a man named, Jesus."*

I remember praying with Nanny and how her prayers made me feel safe. We'd often walk miles through town putting little notes on people's cars that shared the story of Jesus. I loved it and my feet never got tired.

One day, I found the courage to tell Nanny my secret. You might wonder how a little four year-old shares such horror? It was through many tears and the limited vocabulary I had at the time to explain what had happened. I remember distinctly saying something like, "He is putting his mouth on me".

I don't have any memories of how she reacted. All I remember was my mother suddenly being there. I remember her looking down at me saying, "Why are you telling your Nanny such terrible lies? You need to tell her you're lying and apologize!"

I wasn't lying! How could she say I was lying? It was the truth!

Nanny taught us that lying was a sin and telling the truth made God happy! I didn't want to make Jesus unhappy. If I lied I might not be protected like Moses and Joseph. My mother's face scared me, and my body shook with fear. She was here in front of me, and God wasn't. He was invisible, but she could hurt me. I had to make a choice.

"God was invisible; she was here in front of me, and could hurt me!"

I told Nanny I had lied! I remember feeling so sad because I didn't want Nanny to think I was a bad girl. I was afraid she wouldn't love me anymore, and she was all I had.

I have no memory of how Nanny responded to me; I DO remember from that moment on I felt a shame set in that would be with me for most of my life. I was a liar, I was bad, and I was different than everyone else.

Auntie Maude

I remember Mom being gone again. She came and went. I always felt safest when she was gone. Dad was still in prison and I'm sure the burden became too much for Nanny. She was not young anymore.

My Auntie Maude stepped into the picture when I was four. This was my dad's aunt, my grandpa's sister. She was a delightful lady. She didn't tell me stories, but she loved to sew and work in the garden. She was tall and thin with a lot of brown hair piled on top of her head like women wore in the 70's.

"I always felt safest when my Mom was gone."

Auntie Maude was regal and elegant. She had drawers full of jewelry that she'd let me play in all day. I loved her lipstick and handbags. Her hands were always scabbed from working with her roses. Her garden was so big and filled with beautiful colors, exhilarating smells, and lots of bugs.

I loved playing with the roly-poly bugs in her garden. I envied these little blue-gray critters that lived in the garden under rocks. They'd quickly roll into a ball and play dead when danger came, just like I would do when "he" came into my room.

"It wasn't long until another move was made."

I liked watching the snails as they sauntered through the garden wearing their hard-shelled house that they could retreat and hide when they saw danger. They made me laugh, and I would play with them for hours imagining that I could hide from danger as they did.

I had many wonderful memories with my Auntie Maude, but it wasn't long until another move was made, I went to live with my dad's Grandma.

Grandma Robbins

My Grandma Robbins had ears that truly listened, arms that always held, a love that was never ending, and a heart that was made of gold.

When my dad was released from prison, I was just turning five and about to start school. I had to live somewhere and with someone who would be willing and capable to make sure I got to school everyday. I needed someone who could give me structure and routine. Dad was now single, around twenty-four years old, and had no stability in his life. Living with him was not an option. My mom was in Louisiana with her boyfriend.

I moved from Monrovia to Barstow, California. My Great Grandma rose to the charge and offered to be my safe haven and home. I don't ever remember meeting my Great Grandma Robbins until I went to live with her, but I had seen her in pictures holding me as a baby.

Grandma had a nice home, and she lived alone. Her husband had passed so she had plenty of time for me. She was much older than my other grandma, and she was tall and stately. I remember a friendly freckled face with auburn hair.

"I remember a friendly, freckled face with auburn hair."

She loved to play and create things. She taught me how to knit potholders. She taught me to play cards, I could play a mean game of solitaire and knit you an amazing potholder by the time I was six years old.

Grandma's home backed up to the desert, and I spent many hours exploring as though I was on a great adventure. I was prepared with a backpack of water and snacks, and a large stick for battling snakes and scorpions. Thank goodness I never saw one, as I am sure there would have been no battle but screaming and running instead. I just found such joy in pretending. I was a born entrepreneur always looking to create.

I spent many evenings singing Charlie Rich and John Denver songs and playing solitaire at the dining room table.

She always had chores for me, which I was eager to do. She would even trust me with washing the dishes and her precious porcelain coffee cups.

She had many treasures and I spent a lot of time gazing at them. I remember her home being a mansion (through a little girl's eyes)

"I was ... free to let my imagination come alive!"

and in the back of the home there was an open room with a large fireplace and tile floors. I don't remember ever sitting in this room with grandma, but I do remember it as my playroom. I had my own bedroom, and another room was filled with many toys for me to play with.

I was safe and free to let my imagination come alive.

I would drag my little sister into these adventures on a regular basis, some of them she would be so excited for, and others would scare the living breath out of her. One such adventure was my many nightly séances. On these evenings I'd tie a bandana around my head, outline my eyes with dark eyeliner, and sit at a table set up with my dolls. In the center of the table was a hamburger candle that I got in my Happy Meal from McDonalds.

I turned the lights down to an ominous hue and invited my sister to join my dolls and me to call "the dead" back to life. The evenings ended with my sister as white as a ghost, fear stricken, tears rolling down her face as she ran from the room screaming for Grandma to save her.

My grandmother playfully chased me through the house with a flyswatter. She'd eventually catch me, but I didn't mind. My grandmother was my biggest cheerleader and my fiercest protector.

For the very first time in my very young life I began to feel a sense of true safety and comfort. I felt like I belonged somewhere.

I remember these years... being so carefree and full of fun. I made friends in kindergarten. I loved the structure of school and how consistent it was. I loved coming home to my grandma, and how she looked forward to me being there. She always had a snack waiting and I would start my homework. Then I'd get to play, play, play.

"For the very first time in my young life, I began to feel a sense of true safety."

Nighttime was always the hardest time for me. I would crawl into my beautiful bed and after Grandma's kisses and snuggles, I would drift off into my five-year-old little girl dreams. I wished I could dream about bunnies and baby dolls, but that was never the case. I would lie in my bed frightened and believing I could hear footsteps coming down the hall.

I tried to hide my head under my pillow so I couldn't hear them, but the noise would get louder and louder with each step as it got closer and closer to me. Boom, Boom, boom; the steps were heavy and definite. I would plug my ears, but the noise just got louder and louder.

Today I know those footsteps were the sound of my heart beating with anxiety. All those nights I thought it was him coming to carry me off to another room. I'd eventually drift off to sleep and wake up to another beautiful day where no one could hurt me, and I'd bounce off to my kindergarten class without a trouble in the world.

> *"I tried to hide ... so I couldn't hear them, but the noise would get louder & louder!"*

Grandma used to talk to me in the evening while we watched Lawrence Welk and knitted our newest project. Most of our talks were happy and fun but sometimes she would talk about going to heaven someday. These talks made me feel afraid. What would happen to me if she was gone? Who would protect me?

The thought of her not being with me would throw me into a panic and I'd jump from my chair and bury my head in her lap and cry.

I'd beg her not to ever leave me. She would take my face covered in tears, and gently wipe them away. She'd say, "My dear sweet Cathy, I will never leave you, even if you can't see me anymore. I will be with you, I promise."

I couldn't quite understand how that would work but I trusted her more than anyone I'd ever known. This was enough to comfort me. Grandma would always say "I'll protect you from that bad man," she believed me even when I was forced to lie.

Then, suddenly everything changed ... again!

It was all so frantic, and I didn't know what was happening, but I do remember being taken to the neighbor's house in the middle of the night and being forced to eat Frosted Flakes for breakfast the next morning, and they tasted horrible. I was upset and confused.

"Then, suddenly, everything changed ... again!"

The pleasant lady took me to school, but my dad picked me up. "Where is Grandma?" I asked "Why isn't she here to get me? Is she okay, Daddy?"

I felt a familiar fear rise in my belly and the panic set in.

Dad didn't answer until we got back to Grandma's house. He sat me down in the swing in the backyard. He said that Grandma had been taken to heaven. She had died! At that moment a part of me died also. I knew things would never feel the same again.

I was devastated and cried until there were no more tears left.

Sometimes people come into your life for a moment, a day, or a lifetime. It matters not the time you spend with them but how they impact your life in that time - Unknown

I'm suddenly jolted from my daydreaming by a loud shriek from the water. I jump up to rescue my own little one, but then I hear the shriek turns into a vigorous giggle and we all begin to laugh!

"I will pray for them and nurture their souls."

My grandchildren. They're so fun to be with. I can't imagine life without them.

I can't ever promise my grandchildren I won't leave them, but while I'm here, I will give them as many tools to navigate life as I can.

I will share stories of heaven, God, and His son, Jesus. I will tell them of a way that we will be able to spend eternity together. I will pray for them and nurture their souls like my Nanny did. I will spend time teaching them, talking to them, listening and kissing them as my Grandma and Auntie Maude did for me. I will cuddle, kiss boo-boos, and support them any way I can with the time we have together.

These women were enough to give me a foundation of love. They taught me what safety felt like and they instilled in me a belief in God. They prayed for me and fought for me the best they could.

We never know how long we have with those we love, or how we will impact them with the time we have. If you have ten years or only 10 minutes with someone make it mean something. You never know when you might change the course of someone's life

*"You never know
when you might
change the course of
someone's life!"*

Your Notes

Who are the angels in your life? What are their names and what are your memories of them? By remembering these people, we recognize the hand of God in our lives all along:

_____
_____
_____
_____
_____
_____
_____
_____
_____
_____
_____
_____
_____
_____
_____
_____
_____
_____

Middle School

Chapter 3

"He who passively accepts evil is as much involved
as he who helps perpetrate it."
- Martin Luther King

My daughter walks out onto the stage with her classroom. It is her sixth grade graduation celebration. My youngest child, Alexis, is going into Jr. High school. As I watch her move to the center of the stage I am filled with such awe and wonder. I am struck by how excited she is and how connected she is to her small group of friends.

This morning we worked on her hair and makeup making sure it was just right.

She moves closer to the principal and her name is called, her little face filled with excitement as she looks up and takes the small scroll into her hand, a piece of paper that will set her on the way to a new adventure.

I watch her and for a moment I see a strong powerful young lady moving into her own person - a stark contrast to who I was as I think back to my own experience at this precious age ...

That day was like most other days, as I rode in the back of our yellow school bus towards home. I lived in a very desolate part of Haughton, Louisiana where we were five miles from the nearest gas station, and another ten to our town.

The roads were two lane highways that were neatly lined with large oak trees and thick forest on either side. At each stop, I watched kids scramble from the bus with their belongings, excited to be home and out of school for the day.

I wondered what it must feel like to want to go home. Did they have warm cookies and milk to sit down to like I would see on *Leave it to Beaver*? Did someone help them with their homework? Were they out the door to play until they were called in for dinner? Did they all sit at the table together and chat about their day, and laugh at the

"I wondered what it must feel like to want to go home."

funny stories? Did their mom and dad tuck them into bed with a good night story and a kiss? Were they left safely in their bed to dream happy dreams, and then awakened gently in the morning for breakfast? Were they hugged and kissed as they left to start their day?

I knew how things should be because I had a little bit of experience living with my Grandma and watching shows like *Eight is Enough* and *Little House on the Prairie*.

On this day, my school bus arrived home and I breathed a deep sigh that my mother's car was gone, meaning she had left for work. She worked nights and was asleep when we left for school. She was gone by the time we arrived home on most days.

Mom always left notes for us before she left for work.

> *"...or would the note banish me to my bedroom?"*

On some days the notes were almost loving and kind, and on others they doled out punishment and long lists of chores. Would I be able to go outside today and play with a friend, or would the note banish me to my bedroom for the night?

I didn't mind my bedroom as these were the days I would get lost in my imagination for hours playing with my Barbies.

I jumped off the school bus eager to see what the afternoon would hold for me.

Yes! I could go outside after my chores and homework were finished. I rushed to get through them hoping to get a couple hours outside before dark. I loved playing in the woods, riding my bicycle, and climbing trees as high as I could go!

As I was preparing to run out the door, I heard his voice, "Cathy, you missed something come back inside!" He was always home in the evenings. I would always rush to get everything done before he arrived home so he couldn't stop me from going outside.

I knew I hadn't missed anything; I was not that foolish to leave reasons why I had to be at the house alone with him. Unfortunately, I had no choice, so I dropped my head and turned to go back into the house.

He placed me on my bed and took off my panties.

When it was over, I got dressed as fast as I could. I felt so dirty, so ashamed and so confused; but, I buried it all beneath a fake smile and headed out the door to ride my bicycle before it got dark.

The day came to a welcomed end, and I headed off to bed. Did all dads touch their daughters the way I was being touched? I pondered in my childish mind. Was this normal? I wanted so badly to be normal. The shame became more prevalent in my life, as I realized that this was not normal and the things that were going on in my home were bad. I felt dirty. My mother told me it was my fault; I should be ashamed.

"I felt so dirty, so ashamed & so confused."

Was it my fault? Was I doing something to provoke it? On one occasion, when what was happening to us became undeniable, she told me that I must enjoy it or I would have told her sooner!

I had told her multiple times; I had told anyone who would listen when I was little. There were days I truly felt like insanity was taking its toll on my little mind. I didn't know what to do or not to do. I was wrong if I did it right and right if I did it wrong. There was no way to determine the outcome of any given day or situation.

I didn't like it! I hated him; I hated him touching me ... now my body began to betray me as I grew older; but, I would stop it! How dare I even for a second enjoy something he was doing! I was bad; I was nasty! It was my fault! She was right.

I felt so alone, I was having experiences no one my age could understand, and if an adult found out I was surely to be punished. The only place I felt safe anymore was at school.

I watched the kids at school, and everyone looked so happy. I would see parents coming to school for their child's birthday, or a special holiday with cupcakes and treats for the class. I would daydream as to what it would be like to have someone love you so much... to be cherished and honored and celebrated.

"I craved her love ... why did she despise me?"

School became my sanctuary. I studied hard and I got good grades,

I tried to stay out of trouble and be a good girl as to not provoke her hatred but nothing ever worked; nothing I did ever brought me the love I so desperately sought from her. I craved her love, her attention and a soft touch. Why did she despise me so? What had I done to deserve such hate and anger? I would have done anything to just have her love me!

My teachers were always kind to me and celebrated my academic achievements and I appreciated that.

I remember a particularly hard day after an entire night of beatings. I had studied so hard for a test in my English class and participated in every discussion. My teacher knew I had the answers but when the day came for the test, I turned the paper in blank.

"My teacher encouraged me and believed in me."

It was all gone. I had nothing.

This teacher called me back into the room during break and made me sit and take the test again. She encouraged me and believed in me. I told her I couldn't remember anything, but I tried anyway, and she was right I did have it all. I passed the test with an almost perfect score.

This teacher shifted me that day and showed me if I just try a little harder and dig a little deeper, I could succeed! To this day I have never forgotten that moment and use it often to get through hard times.

I wanted friends; I wanted to have sleepovers and to go to football games, but I always felt different, so ugly and so very dirty. I wanted to be like the popular girls, they were loved by everyone, so I paid close attention to what they did and what made them so lovable. These girls were wearing pretty clothes, their hair was the latest fashion, and they wore makeup. I decided I should start doing these things, too.

"I wanted friends ... but I always felt different."

The only clothing I had were clothes that she would buy and bring home for us to wear. I only remember shopping for clothes one time in my childhood. She shopped for us, and she selected styles that were not like the other kids.

I remember once being given bowling shoes to wear as my back-to-school shoes. I didn't know they were bowling shoes at the time, but I did know they were atrocious and ugly. I felt so embarrassed each day as I walked into class, but I had no other option, they were the only shoes I had to wear.

I longed to have my own style, to pick out my clothes, do my makeup and hair like the other girls. It's important for children to have their own style as they begin to separate from their parents and develop into their own uniqueness.

I watched my mother come home many days with bags and bags of beautiful clothes, shoes, makeup ,and perfume. She would pour out her treasures and gush over them. She would try them on and model her perfect outfits for us.

I feigned happiness for her but inside I pined for my own treasures and bags of beautiful items that I could use to change who I was.

"I feigned happiness, but inside I pined ..."

My mother had this unique transformation when she would get dressed up, I watched it happen right in front of me and paid close attention. Her mood before she would start getting dressed would be angry and bitter, but as if by magic she would transform into a kinder person. With each layer of makeup, with each new curl she was happier, and by the time she was done she was a new, more pleasant person standing in front of me. I recall one occasion, feeling brave enough, commenting on how she changed when she was dressed up and she replied, "I feel prettier and therefore I am happier."

So that was the solution: be pretty, be happy!

I was fascinated and motivated to become like her and achieve this level of happiness.

I asked if it would be ok for me to start wearing makeup, and I was denied even mascara until eighth grade. Well, I was no longer mildly interested in being beautiful, I was obsessed and I would begin going to any lengths to attain this level of satisfaction.

My pursuit of beauty began with a little mascara each day.

My mother worked nights, so she was always asleep when we went to school in the morning, and she left for work by the time we arrived home. This gave me the freedom to sneak into her bathroom each morning and use her makeup. I'd finish by spraying myself with some of her cherished Charlie Perfume.

"I would begin going to any lengths to attain this level of satisfaction."

It was working, I was starting to get noticed and the popular girls wanted to know me. I recall on one occasion it was the last day of school and a boy that I had a little crush on said to me, "Wow, you look pretty." I felt something inside of me come alive! It lit a fire in my belly and I was determined to be this new girl every day.

On the bus ride home, I'd sit in the back and pick the mascara off of my eyes and wipe my face clean. Sometimes I'd catch glances of other students watching me, but I had to do whatever it took to not get caught. I was afraid to even imagine what my punishment would be if she caught me.

It wasn't long until I began trying on her clothes at night while she was at work. We were remarkably close in our size. I felt so beautiful in her clothes and makeup. I understood the transformation now; and thus, began the arduous task of wearing her clothes to school every day. I never dared wear anything clean, I would pull from her dirty clothes each morning and shake out the wrinkles and cover the

> *"Each day I would feel the panic set in ..."*

smell of cigarettes with more perfume. I would always take extra clothing in my backpack and change in the bathroom at school before getting on the school bus to go home.

Each day I would feel the panic set in as we rounded the corner to my house. Would I see her car in the driveway? Would she have missed work today for some reason? When I saw the coast was clear my heart rate would subside to normal. I would hop off the bus and run to her bedroom to tuck her clothing back into her hamper.

And then my luck ran out. I rounded the corner that fateful day and there it was - her car in the driveway! I was caught and she gave me one of the most horrific beatings of my life ... one that would shift my little brain forever.

I hear Alexis and her friends as they near the car, they bounce into the back seat chatting about all the excitement of the day. I listened with a joyful heart so grateful that she would never experience the pains that defined my life for so long. That I could give her the attention, the hugs, the kisses and yes, the homemade chocolate-chip cookies that greeted her home that day.

Your Notes

What was your home life like as a child? How about school? What things did you fear? What things became important, and why? Understanding where mental habits started helps us find truth to heal:

_____

_____

_____

_____

_____

_____

_____

_____

_____

_____

_____

_____

_____

_____

_____

_____

_____

_____

A Mother's Hands - A Leather Belt

Chapter 4

"Each day of our lives we make deposits in the memory banks of children."
- Charles Swindoll

Flashback ... Mom's coming, and I want to stop it. I have to stop it! "She doesn't belong here! This is my territory - my world!" I screamed at God! How could they invite her? It's a family reunion combined with birthday celebrations. I love my family and have spent many years making up for lost time with them. I am excited to see everyone until I am told that "she is coming."

We haven't spoken since my wedding in 2015. My family doesn't know this as I am not the kind of person who sows discord in relationships; so of course, they invited her. But now, I am angry.

This anger is an old familiar blanket that I wrapped around my life for many decades. It was a blanket that shielded me from this world of unsafe people. It was an anger that would manifest itself into every relationship and every opportunity that arose. I've carried around resentment, a burning in my stomach, for most of my life. The problem with creating a wall of protection is that it also keeps love out. It blocks us from true intimacy with God and others. It keeps us emotionally isolated and all alone, even when we're with a group of people or a large family.

I felt as if I spent most of my life alone, afraid, hopeless, unloved, and broken beyond repair with a shroud of shame and dirtiness that went with me everywhere.

"The old familiar blanket of anger blocks true intimacy with God!"

Even though she lives 3000 miles away, her ever-present voice quietly whispers her hurtful words day after day.

I was afraid of every hand that ever reached out to me. I would flinch and pull away. Hands became a weapon to me, and not an instrument of love or affection.

I used to love her hands, the way they looked, the way they smelled. They were so soft, and her nails were always done to perfection. Her hands were different than other hands, as she had veiny hands, but I thought they were beautiful. I hoped my hands would be that pretty someday.

The first time I can remember her hand hitting me was around 8 years old. Maybe the reason this is my first memory is because it was less hitting or spanking and more of a beating.

Once the beatings began, her hands began to change, and I became afraid of them. Her hands no longer meant love to me; they always meant anger, rage, and pain. In the beginning I was never sure what would set her off. It could be as innocent as a wrong word, eating something that wasn't put on her approved daily menu, not saying "yes ma'am", or "no ma'am", not standing up straight, or stuttering.

The beatings ranged from a few slaps in the face to hours of torture. It was physical abuse, and lots of it, but the true torture was mental.

"Her hands began to change, and I became afraid of them."

Physical beatings have a way of diminishing, but emotional torture stays with us for a lifetime. Sure, these physical beatings took their toll on my young body, but the bruises have faded. The mental bruising, however, has lived on inside of me for decades.

Some of her favorite things to say to me were:

"You're a split-toothed bitch," as I had a gap between my teeth most of my life that I have since capped because I thought myself so ugly with it.

"Your breasts are pointy and ugly, not pretty like other girls".

"Your eyes are brown because you're so full of shit." I realized at 40 that my eyes were not brown but a beautiful shade of green. Thus, showing how I could believe a lie so very long even when I should have been able to see the truth every time I looked in the mirror - shocking!

The insults continued with:

"You will never be of any value to anyone" ... "Your body is ugly, and you stand funny."

"You talk funny."

"Your hair is stringy."

"You're nothing but a liar."

"We can believe a lie ... even when the truth's staring us in the mirror."

On many nights my mother would come home around midnight with her bottle of Black Tower Wine or Miller Light and drink alone. She would move through the house making sure that all our chores had been done, and check her markings on the food. She marked the milk and counted the bread slices everyday before she left for work.

Two to three times a week she would find a reason to drag us out of bed and scream accusations at us. For hours she would demand to know who ate this, who ate that, why is this cup still dirty, and on and on.

This night was different though. She didn't just wake me up with screaming, she woke me up with her fingers in my hair down to my scalp, and dragged me out of bed. I grabbed my head and screamed as my body fell off the bed and hit the floor. I scrambled to my feet to try to walk. I was sure if I didn't, I was going to lose a large chunk of hair.

> *"This night was different ... I was dragged out of bed."*

I was thrown into a chair. Her face was red, her eyes were glaring, and she was gasping for breath. She moved her face close to mine and said, "Bitch, are you wearing my clothes to school?"

At that moment the blood drained from my body, my heart went cold. I began to tremble and shake, as I formed the word, "No!"

I knew by now it didn't matter if you lied or told the truth, the punishment was the same. I watched her hand suddenly jerk back, and with a full fist she punched me in the face. I was shocked and stunned as I felt a warm trickle down my nose. She's going to kill me!

I crawled to a corner of the room and crouched against the wall with my legs pulled tightly to my chest, my arms wrapped around my knees burying my face to protect it from her flailing fists.

Once she got tired of hitting me, she sat back on her chair and screamed profanities and accusations. She would have stopped sooner if I showed weakness and cried, but I would never let her see me cry. In fact, by this time I was almost forgetting how.

She hurled her insults at me, one after another, "You are ugly, you're a thief, you're going to hell, nobody loves you, and on and on and on. I continued to just stare at her and let no emotion out at all. Inside, I was bubbling with hate and rage, and I wanted to jump from my corner and beat her and hit her and scream how much I hated her. But I couldn't move.

"It didn't matter if you lied or told the truth, the punishment was the same."

Once she realized the screaming and the beatings were not going to get to me, she yanked me by the hair and sat me in the kitchen chair. She left the room and returned with a pair of scissors and a plastic cereal bowl. To my horror she put the bowl on my head and cut my long beautiful blonde hair to match the circumference of the bowl. It was then I cried, and this seemed to satisfy her. She leaned down and whispered into my ear, "You're not so pretty now, are you?"

I thought this would be the end of it, and I could run back to my bed and sob into my pillow. But no. She took me into my bedroom and removed every piece of clothing that I owned, along with my shoes and the precious little makeup I was allowed to wear. She put everything I owned into the backyard in a heaping pile and prepared to burn it.

"It was then I cried; this seemed to satisfy her."

She went into my sister's closet and took out a dress I had passed down to her 3 years earlier, and a pair of house slippers, and said, "This is what you will be wearing to school today."

By now, the sun was starting to rise. I was so tired, and my body hurt from my scalp to the bottom of my feet. I wanted to go back to bed, but it was too late.

She threw the clothing at me and to my horror I knew she was actually going to make me wear it! I plotted my escape in my head. There was no way I would go to school like this. She looked at me with her black eyes and sinister smile and said, "I know what you're thinking, but I'll be standing with you at the bus stop and you will be getting on the school bus."

She broke me. I begged and pleaded with her to stop, but the more I begged, the more pleased she became.

A Mother's Hands - A Leather Belt

We stood at the bus stop together: me in a dress that was so tight I could barely breathe, with sleeves that were supposed to go to my wrists but couldn't make it past my elbows. The dress was so short you could see my panties. I was wearing a pair of old ugly fuzzy slippers. My eyes were swollen and black from crying and being hit, and with my hair so short, my scalp was cold.

I stood there at the bus stop with the other kids. They tried so hard not to stare, and I wanted so badly to just die at that moment. I wished she would have killed me. It would have been better than what I was going through at that moment.

I heard the bus coming around the corner and began to panic and cry. It clamored to a stop in front of us, and I went to the back of the line to get on. I will never forget walking down the aisle of that bus as every head turned to stare at me. I diverted my eyes and would not look at them; I couldn't bear to see their reaction.

"I wanted so badly to just die at that moment."

By the time I made it to the back of the bus that morning, I was a different person. That was the moment when everything inside me shifted, and I felt a hardening inside of my heart! It scared me to feel this way ... I was only twelve!

From the ages of twelve to fourteen, the beatings became more and more severe, thought out, and planned. I knew I would die if I didn't get away.

I found a way. I fled Louisiana at the age of fourteen and made my way to California (continued in another chapter).

Now, here I am thirty-six years later still dealing with an abusive and out of control woman. I believe we all have an enemy of our soul, but I also have an enemy of my life. She prowls around each day looking for ways to infiltrate my fortress of protection from her, up to contacting stepchildren, friends, and whomever will listen to her. She screams from the rooftops how my pedophile is a good man who never did anything wrong, and how I am a vessel of lies and pain for her.

"Everything inside me shifted; I felt a hardening of my heart."

I have tried over these last three decades to extend the hand of forgiveness and reconciliation, only to find myself once again, in an abusive relationship with her. Today she doesn't hit me with her hands, but her verbal assaults are just as painful.

I am now in a place where I have to be in front of her once again. I am panicked and afraid, just like I was back then.

"Lord, how am I to do this and be ok? How can I enjoy my family and still be safe?"

I reach out to a mentor for direction and she asked me if I have ever set clear boundaries with her or had any closure with her at all since our last contact. I consider her question and my response is, "No". Wow! What a concept. I am 49 years old; not 14! I won't cower in a corner anymore! It's time to take my power back, and that's what I did!

I sit down to my computer and I pray, "Lord give me the words. Words that will reflect you; words that are kind yet firm." Within minutes my fingers begin to fly across the keyboard, and within the hour I have a letter penned that will once again shift me forever. But this time the shift is into acceptance of how things are, that I am an adult and I have the right to protect myself from anyone who treats me badly even if it's the woman who gave birth to me.

"I am panicked and afraid - just like back then."

This wasn't easy I had to work on patterns that kept me stuck in old feelings.

By the time the family arrived I was a stronger and healthier version of myself. We were within ten feet of each other and there were no words spoken. It wasn't uncomfortable as one might think. I had a good time despite her presence and truly enjoyed celebrating family!

For so many years even after leaving the home and even three thousand miles away I still allowed her to have hold over me. Setting the boundaries helped me take my power back.

Proverbs 18:21

"Death and life are in the power of the tongue."

Over time I have allowed God's words to flow into my heart and mind telling me who I really am and what my value is. I had to tear down the wallpaper of lies that she attached to me and put up all new wallpaper with His truth.

It takes time, commitment and consistency, but our minds will be renewed.

Romans 12:2

"Be transformed by the renewing of your mind."

Your Notes

Is there anything you fear related to touch? Why? What about someone else's words (lies) in your mind? Are you speaking life over these areas and allowing God's Word to renew your mind?

_____

_____

_____

_____

_____

_____

_____

_____

_____

_____

_____

_____

_____

_____

_____

_____

_____

_____

_____

Candy Cigarettes
& Alcohol
Chapter 5

*"There is no greater inhumanity then
hurting or belittling a child."
- Child insider*

*T*he fall air is crisp in Big Bear today, the trees are just starting to turn, and the leaves burn red and yellow. I can hear the wind blowing, sounding like rushing water as the trees gently bend to the flow of fresh air.

My husband, Adam, unloads the mountain bikes and puts them into our cozy rented cabin that we will call home for the next few days. This is our annual mountain biking trip and this time we are sharing it with some of our closest friends.

I've been doing this trip for eight years now. The ride is easily three hours with over four thousand feet of climbing which might be just another ride for some, but for me it is a tribute to the healthy lifestyle that I have lived since 2007.

As I ascend after departing the lift, my heart begins to pound, and

I can feel the dark recesses of my lungs opening up and welcoming the thin air. My heart pounds in my ears as I breathe deeply. It takes several minutes to adjust but I finally do, and I am hammering along through the pine trees as the familiar scent of dirt hits my nostrils, and small rocks bounce off of my tires.

My lungs and heart are strong, and my peddling comes easier. Soon I am winding through the trails admiring the beauty around me.

I feel so grateful that I am healthy enough to do this ride every year. My journey would have been much different had I continued down the path that it began on ...

I was eleven years old when alcohol and cigarettes were introduced to me by my abuser.

I lived in a home where excessive drinking took place daily and the thick smell of Benson and Hedges cigarettes filled the house regularly. I hated the smell of cigarettes. My mom was a heavy smoker; so was her husband. It was a habit that disgusted me. I had the same kind of aversion towards alcohol. Even at such a young age I never wanted to introduce that substance to my body. I wanted nothing to do with anything that would make people act so badly.

"My journey would've been much different had I continued down the path it began on."

My abuser bribed me with candy to keep his secrets, little did he know by this time his secret was safer than Fort Knox. By now I had been called a liar so many times, that I had given up on telling anyone.

Candy, sugars and any such treats were banned from our home. We were put on strict eating schedules and if there was any deviation from this schedule, a beating would ensue. The food allotted to us daily was not enough to keep a growing child satisfied; so, when I realized that I could get extra food or the prized bar of chocolate if I let him touch me, I began the great game of manipulation that would last decades into my life.

"I would have traded the candy in at any moment for a peaceful day ..."

With each horrible night that went by, came a day of feasting on forbidden foods. I would have traded the candy in at any moment for a peaceful day of love and safety.

It wasn't long until alcohol and cigarettes started to replace the gifts of candy. Unfortuntely, my abuser had found one more way to keep me in his tight grip of secrecy by introducing me to cigarettes and alcohol. I wanted nothing to do with any of it; but, he wasn't suggesting it - he was demanding it! The first time I tried a cigarette my throat burned, my eyes filled up with water and my lungs felt as if they were going to burst. Cigarettes were awful and smelled horrible, but deep in my mind, I felt a little more grown up, which meant I was becoming stronger.

If I was growing up and closer to being an adult, it would mean I could start protecting myself better, and leave home sooner. I needed to be grown up and from that moment on, anything that propelled me closer to that milestone was ok by me.

I started sneaking cigarettes on a regular basis from both adults in the home and smoked them when I was alone. It took several cigarettes and many nauseous moments and gut-wrenching hacking, but finally I started to understand the appeal of these little white sticks that burned fire and smoke. It wasn't long until I was thinking more about them and planning them into my day. I was even becoming so bold that I would get up extra early and sneak a smoke in the morning... until that fateful day.

> *"I started to understand the appeal of those little white sticks."*

I awoke early that Saturday morning to go outside and have a cigarette before anyone woke up.

The night before had been the usual Friday night with mom coming home late with her bottle of Black Tower wine and him up waiting for her with his bottle of Jack Daniels. They drank late into the night and as usual this triggered one of their many brawls that would end with my mom up against the wall and her husband's hands tightly wrapped around her neck speaking these words through clenched teeth and rage in his eyes:

"If you don't shut your mouth, I am going to knock those pearly white teeth right down your throat!"

This was shouted at her on a regular basis, and she would dare him. One of these days I wish you would carry out that threat, I would whisper under my breath and think what she might look like with all her teeth missing.

After these nights, they would both be sleeping well into early afternoon, so I would jump out of my bed, slip on my house shoes and robe, and ever so stealthily I'd sneak out the back door. The door creaked a little, and my heart began to race faster. I stopped to listen for any movement but there was none.

I would tiptoe out the back door and gently close it behind me. Some days I only had a half-smoked cigarette butt that I was able to pull from the large ashtray pile from the night before. I would pull out my lighter and light up my new-found companion. I took that familiar first draw and as I let the smoke

"I would light up a new-found companion."

fill up my lungs and slowly escape through my pursed lips, I would feel the familiar lightheadedness that also came with a little body buzz that I was beginning to enjoy.

I held that half cigarette between my fingers like so many grownups I had watched, I wondered if I looked as cool as they did, I was enthralled by how "adultish" I was starting to feel.

That day I had just bent down to snuff out my little friend when I heard someone coming around the corner. My heart sank, my body began to shake from the inside out, my blood drained from my face as I slowly turned to see her standing there in the shadows.

> *"I was enthralled by how 'adultish' I felt."*

Did she see me smoking? Can I lie? My mind whirls; I feel faint. What would she do?

"What are you doing Cathy?"

I was so afraid. I knew that it wouldn't matter what I said, the punishment was inevitable. Would it be the belt, her hand, a dish, a broom? How will the beating happen this time? I learned that it didn't matter whether I spoke the truth or lied, the pain was coming, so I lied.

In an instant her hand knotted into my hair and she dragged me into the house and threw me into a chair. She screamed and screamed into my face, her breath was hot and foul from a night of drinking and smoking. Her eyes looked dark and demonic, but somewhere in her face I saw amusement, almost delight. It's as if somewhere inside of her she liked this, she lived for it and welcomed it.

She asked me again what I was doing, and once again I replied "nothing." She slapped me in the face, my head spins from the impact, stinging my cheeks. She continued to ask, and I continued to deny I was smoking. She threw me out of the chair onto the floor and started to kick me. I rolled into a ball trying to protect my face. She yanked me up off of the floor by the hair and threw me against the wall, "You're a liar," she screamed, "I hate liars, I hate you!"

"I waited for what seemed like forever for the punishment to come."

She asked me again what I was doing and this time I succumbed to the beatings. I admitted I had smoked a cigarette. I looked up to see her countenance change; she became calmer, but this calm is not the calm after the storm, it is the quiet eerie silence that comes right before the storm. The amusement on her face is like that of a serial killer who had subdued their victim and is mentally preparing the kind of torture that will follow.

I crawled up into the large chair above me and waited for what seemed like forever for the punishment to come. What would it be this time? Would I be beaten more; would she kill me this time for sure?

I watched her walk away and come back with a full pack of cigarettes. She placed them on the table next to me and pulled one out, she looked at me and said, "Eat it."

My eyes grew big as saucers the tears welled up. She proceeded to tell me not only was I to eat it, but I was to swallow it. Her eyes glowed with amusement.

I placed the first cigarette into my mouth and took a bite, my mouth burned, and my throat closed. I couldn't get enough saliva into my mouth to swallow them. She screamed into my face, "Swallow them!"

"I'll teach you to never want to smoke again!"

I tried so hard to hold the tears back, I would never allow her to see me cry, but my eyes betrayed me, and the water began flowing down my soft pink cheeks. I finally swallowed that first cigarette, now I just had to keep it down and not let her see my body try to reject it. My stomach wretched, I began to gag as the small pieces of paper and tobacco made its way into my stomach.

> *"The water began flowing down my soft, pink cheeks."*

After four hours of torture and half a pack of cigarettes she gave up. I couldn't get any more down and I think she was growing tired and bored, so she let me into the bathroom where I threw up for the next two hours.

I made my way to my bed where I buried my face into my pillow and sobbed. Why was this my life, God where are you? I didn't leave my room that day and thankfully she was too hung over to inflict any more of her torture.

The next question might be, "Wow, I guess you never smoked another cigarette again?"

No, I smoked for twenty-seven years after that.

"Drugs and alcohol became my refuge."

Not only did I become a smoker, but by the time I was sixteen, I was a meth addict. The warm arms of drugs and alcohol became my refuge for the next couple decades.

And then, things started to shift. At thirty-eight I was having trouble catching my breath after going up the stairs in my home. I knew I couldn't continue smoking - it was going to kill me!

My first Grandson was born in 2006 and as I watched this beautiful new life come into the world, I knew I had to make a change if I wanted to see him grow up.

I made a New Year's resolution to quit smoking, for the fifth year in a row. This was going to be the year that I would be successful! By the time December 31st rolled around my ashtray was laden with cigarette butts falling over all sides. I had smoked more in the last week then I had smoked in the last year. I was going to miss them, I knew that, but I could not go on this way any longer.

I had tried the patch, gum, only smoking on weekends I even went to the length of being hypnotized, nothing ever worked for long. In fact, there were times that I would be wearing the patch while chewing the gum and smoking, I was hopelessly addicted.

January 1st, I took that ashtray filled with cigarette butts and I put them in a mason jar, I filled the jar with water and put it in the cabinet. This was a suggestion given to me by my Aunt, she told me to go stick my nose in that jar every time I wanted a cigarette and the smell would be so bad that the urge would go away, it sounded silly and too easy, but I was desperate.

"I had tried everything; I was hopelessly addicted!"

I had tried everything else. "Why not this", I said to myself.

I also knew that in order to quit smoking I would have to lay down the alcohol. They were like peanut butter and jelly, they just went together. The plan was to quit drinking for one year and then once I was cigarette free, I could begin drinking again.

I never believed alcohol was a problem for me, yes maybe I blacked out sometimes, woke up in my own vomit and acted foolishly but didn't everyone when they drank? My drinking was nothing compared to theirs.

I remember waking up January 1st, 2007 feeling hungover from cigarettes and alcohol not sure which was making me the sickest. This sickness carried me through for a few days, until January 6th to be exact. I didn't even have to use the mason jar filled with molding and wet cigarette butts. Wow, maybe I had this for the first time!

"Maybe I had this for the first time ..."

Or maybe I didn't! I had been invited to a wedding anniversary celebration of a dear friend.

I thought I was strong enough that I could do this! I wasn't, I drank a martini and smoked a cigarette!

I felt defeated and hopeless; I would never change.

You know what? I was right! I could not change; not on my own anyway.

That very next night I walked through the doors of Celebrate Recovery at the church I had been attending. I had walked by their booth many times on my way in and out of Sunday services and I wanted to go pick up literature, but I was too embarrassed to be seen doing so. I even attended one of their meetings earlier that year but the holidays were fast approaching, how do you not drink during the holidays?

I was scared and felt like I would be judged, I had never been fully transparent at church! At church when asked if I was ok, I said "Yes, I am great ... How are you?" Every time!

If people saw me coming into this group, they might think I had problems, that I was broken, they might find out that I smoked cigarettes and drank alcohol!

I worked so hard to make my life look good on the outside to avoid judgment or rejection! I wanted so badly to fit in and be loved!

I came in late and sat by myself in the back; but, instead of leaving early like I had planned, I attended the Newcomers group. I was desperate;

> *"I wanted so badly to fit in and be loved!"*

maybe this would help me. There were seven to eight people sitting in a circle.

The leader started off with a reading of what Celebrate Recovery was about. They said this was a spiritual-based recovery program that helped with all different kinds of habits, hurts and hang-ups and that there was anonymity, meaning no one would know besides them that I was coming to the group. I was intrigued. I had all those things: hurts, habits and hang-ups. My spirit quickened and I began to listen more intently.

After the readings it was time to go around the circle and introduce ourselves. We started out with our name and then our reason for coming.

My heart raced, what would I say? I wasn't sure who or what I was. I thought maybe co-dependent or just addicted to cigarettes, my heart beat faster now as it came to my turn.

"My spirit quickened and I began to listen more intently."

Then suddenly, without any forethought or planning, my mouth opened and I said, "Hello, my name is Catherine and I am an alcoholic."

What did I just say!! I did not consider myself an alcoholic!!!

I wasn't drinking out of a paper bag under a bridge! I didn't even drink every day. Well, I had said it, and in an instant, I felt a burden so heavy and so overwhelming lift from my body that is hard to describe.

I stayed at Celebrate Recovery for the next five years and served in many capacities. And you know what? My year passed without having a cigarette, and when that year came to an end, I no longer wanted to drink. My life had been spun on its axis that first night, and it has never been the same.

In the rooms of recovery, I found a family. A family of broken people who supported each other and carried each other's burdens.

A family who knew all of me and still loved me. I also found 12 steps to live life by. Steps to help me get honest, learn how to surrender to God, clean up the wreckage of my past, make amends to the people who suffered as a result of my bad choices. Steps that teach me to look at my part, and finally steps that take me out of myself and give me the freedom to see the needs of others.

"In the rooms of recovery, I found a family."

I hear the wind begin rushing through my ears as we start the descent of the mountain. I hear my husband's faint voice asking about our dinner plans and I giggle to myself the simplicity of his life compared to how complex my thinking is.

These bike rides remind me of life sometimes.

We begin our journey and we're unsure how or where to start. Then, as we begin climbing the first hill we come to, we ponder if we're on the right path?

It seems so hard. Did I take a wrong turn or read the map wrong? We continue and then suddenly we are at the top of the hill and the beauty of God's fullness shines around us.

As we stop to take in the breathtaking scenery we see the full picture and determine this was the right path as we can see life now from a 360° view.

We continue on our journey, and as we begin the descent, it makes the climb so worth it. We coast through life for a little while. But just as suddenly, we round a corner and are faced with another hill ... and this one seems so much steeper.

"Oh God No! Please not another climb!"

But you know what I have come to learn about the climbs? They are never as steep as they look from a distance. Once we begin the climb, the hill seems to flatten out a little. Then, once we begin the descent, we are stronger because of our last climb. Every hill we come to gets easier and easier. Don't come to the hills and stop. Don't turn around and go backwards either. Face the climb with Jesus, and each hill will make you stronger.

"Don't come to the hills of life and stop, turnaround, or go backwards."

It is on the climbs that our faith muscle is strengthened, and before you know it, you will be hitting a descent sweeter and more beautiful than the last.

Your Notes

What addiction have you overcome/are you overcoming? Who's your recovery family? What new climb are you facing; and, are you facing it with Jesus?

_____

_____

_____

_____

_____

_____

_____

_____

_____

_____

_____

_____

_____

_____

_____

_____

_____

God, Can You Hear Me?

Chapter 6

"One's dignity may be assaulted and vandalized, but it can never be taken away unless surrendered."
- Unknown

Today I celebrate my third wedding anniversary to Adam, a man who keeps me safe, doesn't judge me, and allows me to be all that I need to be, even if it makes him a little uncomfortable. This is my third marriage and my last. I've spent several years working on myself before I entered this covenant. I would have rather been single then in another relationship that wasn't everything I was looking for. I have settled and cheated myself way too many times to let it happen again.

My life has been a revolving door of dysfunctional relationships, and that's because of my own sickness within me. Nothing changes on the outside until we change on the inside. No man, no house, no car, no bank account will ever give us the happiness we seek until we turn our eyeballs inside.

I learned in my early years that my body could be a very manipulative tool. I learned how to get mostly all I wanted by using it.

Sex was never out of love, it was out of necessity. It was a way to a means.

I lived most of my life afraid of men or belittling them. I looked at them as weak and incapable of true love and commitment. I was certain they were going to eventually hurt me, betray me, or abuse me; so, I took what I could as fast as I could.

In my need to protect myself I became very controlling in my relationships. I made the decisions and I could never be wrong. I was defensive and angry most of the time. I emasculated most of the men in my life by stripping them of dignity and value. It left them feeling empty and worthless.

"Nothing changes on the outside until we change on the inside."

Was this because I was a bad person, or an evil person bent on hurting others? No, this was a taught behavior, and I was a very good student.

The Trip to Mississippi

I was thirteen years old when the abuse escalated on all levels. As my body began to change, the sexual advances were becoming more invasive. My mother began sending me on out-of-state trips with my abuser. I believe it was her way of getting rid of me and not dealing with my escalating rebellion.

Leaving my mother was a relief, even though I knew I would pay for it by being alone with him. Sometimes I didn't know what was worse, but what I did know was that his abuse was usually over more quickly. Her abuse could go on for hours and hours.

One trip I recall most vividly was to Mississippi ...

After arriving in Mississippi, I found myself in a little construction trailer. My step dad was an oil man and we were way out in the middle of nowhere on an oil rig. I saw a lot of men walking around. There was so much activity, maybe he would be too busy to bother with me I hoped.

"At least his abuse was over more quickly than my mother's."

I walked in and looked at my surroundings. It had a small refrigerator, a fold-out table, a small kitchenette, and a couch that rolled into a bed. One bed.

My stomach dropped.

All these years the abuse had been oral, but I knew he was ready to take it further. He talked about it often and shared how he was going to make me an amazing woman and wife for someone someday.

"I don't want to be a wife", I would scream silently to myself. "I hate you, and I hate what you do to me".

I put down my bag and waited.

To my surprise he said he needed to leave and check on his crew. I felt a small sense of relief wash over me.

It wasn't going to happen right now!

I sat on the couch and pulled out my escape, my *Nancy Drew Mystery* book. These books were my drugs in my early years. I escaped into those pages and was whisked off to another world; a world where the women were smart and strong. A world where nothing got by Nancy. She solved every mystery and brought peace into the chaos.

"My body began to tremble; the bile of fear hurt my stomach."

I wanted to be her!

I'm not sure how much time had passed but the sun was getting lower and I began to wonder how much longer I had before he returned. I was hungry, but I knew he would not let me eat until he was satisfied. Food was another way for him to have control, he would withhold meals until his needs were met.

I heard his heavy boots come up the metal steps. My body began to tremble, and the bile of fear hurt my stomach.

The door opened, and I smelled the familiar scent of Jack Daniels whiskey on his breath. His eyes were bloodshot red, and he had a crooked smirk on his face.

"Are you ready to become a woman?" he asked. I wish you were dead, I responded in my head.

I just sat there and waited.

He placed himself on the couch beside me and pulled me closer, his breath was hot and foul, and I avoided his disgusting stare.

"God, please help me if you're there."

He moved closer and put his mouth on my lips, I couldn't breathe. I kept trying to pull away, but he wouldn't let me. He finally pushed back, and began removing my clothes, and his own.

I was paralyzed! It was going to happen and there was nothing I could do to stop it.

I lay back, closed my eyes, and cried out, God please help me if you're there. Please help me!

I couldn't look at him. I couldn't stop it physically, but I could escape mentally. I learned how not to be in a room, even when I was.

I drifted off to my Grandma's house and sat with her making potholders and laughing at the funny antics of *Maude* on the television.

Suddenly, he sat back against the couch and said, "Looks like the Lord doesn't want me going this far, yet!" I jumped off of the couch, grabbed my clothes, and quickly put them back on (we'll talk more about this in a later chapter).

God, you heard me! You are really there! Thank you God, for hearing me!

He tried two more times on this trip with the same result each time and each time he would say the same thing, "I guess God doesn't want me to go that far."

As a result of these crimes against my body and my soul, I couldn't believe in love. I couldn't love myself and I definitely couldn't love anyone else. Love didn't resonate with me *"Love didn't resonate with me ..."* because I didn't have a point of reference. Love was just a word.

I hated myself for decades for all the things they did to me. I hated myself for not trying harder to stop it ... for not continuing to scream out until someone finally listened.

I hated myself for being ugly and stupid, and for being a child that not even a mother could love.

I was broken and in pain. As a result, I chose men who were broken and in pain. I chose men who were emotionally unavailable as I was. I chose controlling abusive men who lied to me and men who told me I had no value.

I believed their lies about who I was until I was in so much emotional pain that I only had two choices ... die, or find a new truth. I chose the daunting work of change! Going through the recovery for the last two decades, I have been exhausted and at times I have felt like nothing would ever change.

"Going through recovery has been exhausting - I chose the daunting work of change."

I have been in a growth pattern for a long time, and it has not been a perfect recovery. Many times I've just thrown my hands up and said, "This is as good as its going to get; I can't dig into this mess anymore".

But something inside of me would never let me stay still for long. I have always had this fire in my belly, knowing there must be more.

We are never standing still, we are either moving forward or backward, I never want to go backwards. So, I pull myself up and I remove the next layer of the onion and get to work.

The woman I am today is a living example of God's merciful grace, but it is also a testimony to what can change when we choose to move, when we choose to be uncomfortable for a little while, and when we choose to surrender our way for God's way.

Today I am a loving and kind partner. I rarely demand my own way, and when I do fall into old behaviors, I apologize. My husband gave me the best compliment I have ever received

> *"Today, I am a living example of God's merciful grace."*

from anyone - it was a comparison to the Proverbs 31 woman:

> "A wife of noble character who can find?
> She is worth far more than rubies.
> Her husband has full confidence in her
> and lacks nothing of value.
> She brings him good, not harm,
> all the days of her life.
> She selects wool and flax
> and works with eager hands.
> She is like the merchant ships,
> bringing her food from afar.
> She gets up while it is still night;
> She provides food for her family
> and portions for her female servants.
> She considers a field and buys it;
> out of her earnings she plants a vineyard.
> She sets about her work vigorously;

her arms are strong for her tasks.

She sees that her trading is profitable,

and her lamp does not go out at night.

In her hand she holds the distaff

and grasps the spindle with her fingers.

She opens her arms to the poor

and extends her hands to the needy.

When it snows, she has no fear for her household;

for all of them are clothed in scarlet.

She makes coverings for her bed;

she is clothed in fine linen and purple.

Her husband is respected at the city gate,

where he takes his seat among the elders of the land.

She makes linen garments and sells them,

and supplies the merchants with sashes.

She is clothed with strength and dignity;

she can laugh at the days to come.

She speaks with wisdom,

and faithful instruction is on her tongue.

She watches over the affairs of her household and

does not eat the bread of idleness.

Her children arise and call her blessed;

her husband also, and he praises her:

"Many women do noble things,

but you surpass them all."

Charm is deceptive, and beauty is fleeting;

but a woman who fears the Lord is to be praised.

Honor her for all that her hands have done,
and let her works bring her praise at the city gate."
Proverbs 31:10-31

I pray every day to be more like her.

God has heard me, and He has cried with me. When I was ready to change, His hand was held out to me, and He has made my burdens light!

"We are never standing still; we're either moving forward or backward."

Your Notes

When's a time you remember crying out to God for help? How'd He answer? Because of His merciful grace, who are you today?

_____
_____
_____
_____
_____
_____
_____
_____
_____
_____
_____
_____
_____
_____
_____
_____
_____

Little Runaway
Chapter 7

"You took away my innocence, but you can never take away my spirit to survive."
- Unknown

I have been a runner most of my life. Living in a home filled with many horrors had lended itself to a very extensive imagination. I would imagine running away and being found by new parents who would love and protect me.

These fantasies soon became my reality as I would begin to run away every day in some fashion.

The hiding began at a very young age. I remember being great at hiding, if I hid, no one was going to find me, and they rarely did. There were times I would hide under the bed. I felt safe under my bed. I became a master at quieting my breath and slowing down my heart as I was sure everyone could hear it as loudly as I could.

I planned my escape by day, and at night, I'd get out of bed and pack a small suitcase. I left my house and walked the streets until dawn. I would then hurriedly return home, stow away my suitcase filled with clothes, snacks, and of course my beloved barbie dolls. I climbed into bed as if I had been there all night. These little trips to nowhere became a way for me to have some control over my life. It was a way for me to feel free.

There were times when I felt scared and wanted to disappear, so I would hide in cars in the middle of the school day. I looked for unlocked cars in the parking lot and then climbed into the backseat.

Sometimes, I drifted off to a world of fantasy, imagining that I was on my way to a great destination. Or other times I would just sleep. I would be awake by the sound of my name.

"The hiding began at a very young age"

I squished myself onto the floorboard of the backseat as far down as I could get and eventually they would stop looking for me.

Sometimes I'd hide in trees, my friends' closets, in sheds or garages. By the time I was thirteen I had run away at least twenty-five times.

Toward the end of my running career, I was introduced to Johnny Grey Jones Detention Facility.

My mom was aware that as I grew older her hold on me was beginning to slip. I truly was a person with nothing to lose, and the rebellion began to rise up along with all the new hormones raging through my body.

I didn't hit or yell at her, but the rebellion was growing, and she could see it.

> *"I wouldn't give her the satisfaction of knowing she was hurting me."*

I imagine she must have wondered how all this was going to play out once I was bigger than her or as strong as her. Surely, she didn't think she could continue these beatings without me; at some point, returning fire.

One evening she went into another rage, I can't remember what started this one. I couldn't keep track of the rules anymore, so I was constantly breaking them.

This particular evening, I watched as she picked up the phone. To my horror, she called the police and asked them to come and arrest me. What?! Arrest me? "For what?" I screamed to myself! I began to sob and begged her to stop, but she hung up the phone, sat down on the couch, and waited.

I ran to my room and cried silently. I would not give her the satisfaction of knowing she was hurting me.

The police arrived and she told tell them I was incorrigible; I was sneaking cigarettes, and stealing her clothes, and a chronic run away.

She said I was a rebellious child and needed to be shown what life would be like if I continued down that road.

"A few nights in juvenile hall might be just what you need!" She said.

I looked up at the officer with sheer terror in my eyes begging him silently to ask more questions, to see the truth that she so carefully hid behind her perfect makeup and hair, but no one could see through the mask she wore so well. The officer looked at me with no compassion at all, and asked if I had a bag to take with me.

"I looked up at the officer with sheer terror in my eyes."

I couldn't believe this was happening! I was a child, not a criminal who needed to be arrested! They were the criminals! You should be arresting them! But I didn't say a word, and I slowly shook my downcast head, no.

The officer looked at her and asked her to put a few items together for me. She walked into the kitchen pulled out a paper grocery bag and filled it to the top with a few items of clothing and my toothbrush. She handed it to me with a look of satisfaction and showed us out the door. I glanced up at her as tears rolled down my face. I hoped somewhere deep inside she was bluffing and would stop this.

She gazed back at me, and all I saw was the evil in her eyes. She looked pleased with herself, and I knew at that moment she hated me!

It was dark outside as I rode in the backseat of that police car. I was petrified, but even then, a sense of relief washed over me as we drove away from the house. The officer said I was being taken to a facility that held teenagers for seventy-two hours until they went to court. The judge would decide my fate at that time.

The drive seemed like an eternity, but they finally pulled up in front of a large old house in the middle of the woods. The worn gray sign that hung above the door read Johnny Gray Jones Youth Shelter and Detention Center.

"The judge would decide my fate."

There was nothing around us. The sky was black, the trees were huge, and this house looked straight out of one of my *Nancy Drew Mysteries*. I was becoming less afraid and more intrigued.

The officer took my bag, and I followed him through a large door into a living room with a desk and chairs. The woman sitting behind the desk had a kind look on her face and my fear began to melt away.

She took my information, said goodbye to the officer, and showed me up a long stairway to a big open room with two rows of twin beds going down each side of the room. Some of the beds were plain and white but others were personalized with stuffed animals and other personal effects.

A strange sensation of peace came over me. I was shown to one of the plain bunks and was told I could put my stuff in the little nightstand next to the bed. The kind lady looked down at me. Her eyes were soft and full of questions, but she didn't ask. She told me to get some sleep and in the morning she would go over the rules of the house. I crawled into bed without looking at anyone, and for the first time I went to sleep feeling safer than I ever had.

> *"Shame had become my friend - connecting was almost impossible."*

I awakened to the sound of muffled yawns, the shuffling of covers, and the faint smell of food cooking. It reminded me of being with my Grandma and how her house would smell in the morning. I pushed back my covers and sat up to see several girls walking to the bathroom. I said hello and dropped my head.

Shame had become my friend and connecting with girls my age was almost impossible. I always felt so different and I never knew what to say to anyone.

I made my way to the bathroom and prepared myself for the day. I headed down the stairs with the rest of the girls towards the smell of breakfast. I entered the kitchen and came upon another kind woman. Wow, is this jail?

I grabbed my breakfast and sat down to eat, it was good and warm. At home, I only had cold cereal breakfasts, so this was a treat.

Afterwards, I went into an office where two women began asking questions. "Why do you feel the need to be running away so often? What is going on in your home that you are trying to get away from?

I told them my mother was beating me, but I never said a word about him. I shook in my chair, holding it in, but I so badly wanted to scream out, "He's hurting me, he is touching me, he wants to have sex with me!"

"I so badly wanted to scream out … but, I couldn't."

But I couldn't! I was afraid I would get in trouble. I was afraid they would blame me just as she had. Telling on her should be enough. Surely, they will do something about the beatings and then it will finally be over!

After our talk they shared the rules of the house and told me I would be in court in front of a judge in two days and my mother would be there. Fear rushed through my body like I had felt so many times before.

The first two days, I followed the house rules and enjoyed every minute. I felt so safe. I even allowed myself to make a new friend. I shared with her the abuse of my step father and she genuinely felt sorry for me. She had gotten in trouble using drugs, but her parents had been good to her and never hurt her. They wanted her to come home and be with them.

I couldn't understand why she was so rebellious. If I had parents that were kind to me I would have never done anything they didn't want me to do; or so I thought in my thirteen year old mind.

On the third day, I stood in a courtroom in front of a judge. There she was. I avoided her eyes.

He didn't come with her and that intrigued me. He had used the ploy of protecting me from her if I would give into his advances. Of course, he didn't show up, he was a coward and a liar.

"To my dismay, they sent me home with my mother."

I don't remember much from that morning as my head spun and I sweated profusely. Would I go to juvenile hall or home? If juvey was like the detention home, then let's go.

But, to my dismay, they sent me home with my mother. I wasn't shocked ... she was a master manipulator and could spin a pretty convincing web of lies.

After returning home from Johnny Grey Jones, I ran away several more times. Each time I called the police reporting that I was a runaway just so I could go back, I wanted to live at Johnny Grey Jones. Each time I would go in front of the judge and get sent right back home.

Well, until the last time ...

Your Notes

Ever wish you could run away from a situation in life? What was/is it? Ever want so badly to talk about how you were being hurt or who was hurting you? Did fear/does fear stop you?

_____

_____

_____

_____

_____

_____

_____

_____

_____

_____

_____

_____

_____

_____

_____

_____

_____

Finally Free
Chapter 8

*"Refuse to inherit dysfunction. Learn a new way of
living instead of repeating what you lived through."*

I don't remember how many times I had been in and out of
Johnny Gray Jones, this time I think the plan was to hold me
longer to determine what was really going on. My step dad started
coming to visit, he brought me my stuffed animals for my bed, and
he'd bring me cigarettes and candy. Looking back, I know he was
afraid I was going to tell.

Unfortunately, at thirteen I didn't know that sexual molestation
was a crime that handed down a pretty stiff sentence. I thought I
was the one who was going to get into trouble.

I did stay longer this time, and I wouldn't get in front of the judge
until the end of the week. I was in heaven. I connected with a couple of girls swapping horror stories about what was happening
in their lives and mine. There was a kinship with these girls. We
etched our names in the closet with the date and a little heart. At

that time I didn't realize things were really going to change for me.

It was a Wednesday night and we were shuttled to church, I loved church! I would get on the Sunday school buses all by myself at home and be off to church and return before anyone woke up. I loved the stories of Jesus, and I always got candy from my Sunday School teacher for memorizing my bible verse.

Some of the other girls weren't as excited, but they got to leave the house. The other girls couldn't understand why I loved this place so much as they couldn't wait to get

"I just wanted to be safe."

back on the streets. I never wanted to do anything bad I just wanted to be safe.

We spent time in the bathroom together getting ready, sharing makeup and clothes. We didn't go outside much at JGJ, but when I did, I was reminded once again of one of the many *Nancy Drew Mysteries* that I had drowned myself in over the years. The dark house shrouded by large trees that dripped long branches down over the ever so large and expansive property. That's how Nancy would have described it. On this night, the moon was brighter than usual, making everything look even more ominous. My imagination ran wild with stories about the dark. *The Mystery of the Moss-Covered Mansion*; *The Hidden Staircase*; *The Mystery at Lilac Inn*. We had enjoyed so many years together, Nancy and I, as we solved mystery after mystery and rescued people from their desperation and despair!

The drive to the church was quite a distance; I had never realized how far out into the dense woods of Louisiana I was.

We made our way inside and were instructed to take a seat in the pews and wait for the service to start. As I sat there, I looked around at all the people and then back to our hodgepodge group of girls. Some of our girls looked downright scary and mean. I could see the uncomfortable glances by the "Church People", but I didn't care.

"I was excited - and scared - but, I knew I had to do it."

One of the girls sitting next to me said, "Hey, that girl is going to run tonight." She poked the girl, Sam, in front of me and whispered, "Hey you gunna run tonight?" She whispered back, "Yes!"

Immediately the words rolled out of my mouth "I want to run with you." She said "Ok, do everything I do."

I was shaking with adrenaline. I was excited and scared, but I knew I had to do it. I knew they were going to send me back home again, and I couldn't go back. I couldn't take another minute in that house. I had no other choice.

As the music began to play, Sam began raising her hands in the air and danced around; she beckoned for me to do the same. This was some of that funny stuff people did in church when they sang. I would see it on my many trips to Sunday school. I copied her right through three songs.

We sat for the message, my mind a whirlwind of thoughts and anticipation. What was next? The Pastor began the message, but all I could hear was my heartbeat in my ears. My body shook and my mind swam with excitement.

Soon the message was over and there was a different gentleman on stage asking people to turn their hearts over to Jesus. MY HEART WAS GOING TO EXPLODE!

> *"As soon as they did, she grabbed my arm."*

I was still shaking with adrenaline when the Pastor asked all those who had accepted Jesus into their hearts to get up and go to the back of the room, and that's when it happened.

She got up!

I started to shake harder. I got up, too.

Sam was walking in front of me, we stepped out of the main sanctuary into a large hall. The group of people we were with turned to the left. As soon as they did, she grabbed my arm with a death grip, looked at me square in the eyes, and whispered through clenched teeth:

"RUN!"

And I ran! I ran faster than I had ever run in my life! I was running FOR my life. The only person I could count on anymore was me.

We exited out of the bright hallway into a dimly lit parking lot. We looked right and we looked left and all options were the same, Louisiana swamp land and dense forest on all sides.

"The only person I could count on anymore was me."

We had to stay as far off the main road as much as possible. We sprinted towards the large dense thicket of trees. I was exhilarated and filled with adrenaline. The only fear I felt was the fear of getting caught, nothing else. I could just sense something was going to be different this time.

I could hear people screaming for us, "Come back! This isn't the answer!" As their voices grew fainter, my fear of being caught began to subside.

I noticed my surroundings and how very dark it was. But the moon was the brightest I had ever seen. Its brilliant light guided our path through the night.

My shoes were full of mud, and my jeans were snagged from crawling over and under barbed-wire fences. It seemed like hours until we finally came upon a large open area. There were piles of rocks and sand hills that touched the sky. Around these large mounds of sand, it looked like water motes or rivers of oil, and in front of that were rows of white trucks.

Sam looked at me and said, "We are going to steal a truck to get us to Shreveport." I was hesitant, but I knew we couldn't keep going on foot.

To our surprise each truck had keys in the ignition! We tried the first vehicle, but it would not start, none of them started. We cursed out our frustration and continued off on foot.

"It was still dark with no hint of daylight ..."

It wasn't long before we came to a two-lane highway, lined with thick trees on both sides. We lay in the ditch looking down both lanes. My breathing became labored again as I feared a police car would be headed down that road any minute, searching for us.

I could not gauge how far we had come, it was still dark with no hint of daylight in the sky. Through the dense forest, we noticed a light on; and we realized there was a house tucked back on the other side of the road. We saw two cars in front of the house.

Sam looked at me and shared her plan. "We'll go to the house," she says, "If they are elderly people, we will tie them up and steal their car."

If I said I was horrified, I don't think that would describe adequately how I felt at that moment. I looked at her and emphatically said, "NO! "We will not hurt anyone."

"We'll tell them we're running away from an abusive facility where they are beating us and raping us. We will ask them to help us." She was not so convinced this would work, but without an accomplice she was at my mercy. We made our way to the home and rang the doorbell. I looked at my clothes; they were ripped and muddy. I must have looked a fright because she did.

The porch light flickered on and a woman's face peeked from behind the window at us. She looked

"The home felt warm and safe ..."

friendly enough; maybe this would work. We yelled from the porch that we needed help. They opened the door and let us in. We proceeded to tell them our concocted story, and sure enough, they believed us.

I remember sitting in their kitchen and a checkered tablecloth draped across an oval table. The home felt warm and it smelled like freshly made biscuits. There were two men and an elderly lady, and they all seemed pleasant enough.

I lied straight to their face about JGJ, I felt bad because I loved it there.

One of the men said he would take us to Shreveport which was about forty-five miles away, he instructed us to hop in his truck. I had heard stories about taking rides from strangers and I felt a little uneasy but not enough to stop me.

"I felt a little uneasy, but not enough to stop me."

It was a very quiet ride. Not much was said by anyone.

He pulled up to the front of the apartments where Sam's boyfriend lived, and he gave us twenty dollars each!

We made our way to her boyfriend's apartment. She assured me we would get help from him. "He will do anything for me." she said.

We knocked on his door and waited for what seemed like forever before the door was opened.

Immediately, I knew things were not going to be as easy as she said. The look on his face was pure shock that turned to anger. Fear overtook me and I began to plead with God not to send me back!

Her boyfriened told us to get the hell out. She begged him to talk to her and He finally agreed. She asked if I could stay at his house while they talked, and he said "No". He demanded that I leave.

About this time the neighbors began to hear the commotion and opened the front door to see what was going on. They inquired as to whether we were ok. My new partner in crime told them she was talking to her boyfriend and asked if I could sit with them until she was done.

Surprisingly, they said yes!

> *"I felt numb; my ears rang with the sound of my own breath."*

The home belonged to two women who looked as if they could be sisters. I began sharing our made-up story about Johnny Gray Jones, how they were beating us and raping us and we just had to escape! You could tell they believed every word as their face showed their horror the longer I spoke. The women asked me to sit down while they talked.

I sat quietly in the small dining room in a wooden rocker. My back was to the kitchen and I was facing the living room. I watched as the animated chatter went on.

"What were they talking about?" I wondered. "Were they thinking of a way to get rid of me?"

I felt numb and my ears rang with the sound of my own breath. The adrenaline was pumping through my body so fiercely that my skin felt like small needles were poking me.

I began to hear noise outside. One of the women went to the window and looked through the curtain when suddenly there was a knock on the door.

I froze.

One of the women opened the door and I heard a man's voice. "Hello Ma'am ... We are looking for two young female runaways." This was it, I was going back!

To my surprise the women did not say anything about me! They acted as if they were clueless and expressed their concern that these young girls be found. Then I heard the man say, "Can I come in and use your telephone?"

I felt the bile rise to my throat, as surely as I sat there, I knew I was going to vomit right on the floor. Large tears pooled in my eyes as he walked through the front door. He came in and was directed to the phone on the wall behind me. His eyes immediately fell on me,

"Large tears pooled in my eyes as he walked through the front door."

I looked away quickly as to not reveal the fear that must have been written all over my face. As I prepared to stand up and leave with him he walked right past me and picked up the phone!

"What was happening?" I screamed to myself!

I didn't dare look at him, I just sat in my chair and prayed! Please God, if you can hear me, do not let them take me back to them!

I heard the man begin to talk on the phone, I could not hear his

"Please God, don't let them take me back."

words as he spoke in a whispered tone, and then I heard, "Ma'am, "Ma'am"... Was he talking to me? Oh my God, he was! What did he want?

My voice wasn't going to work, he was going to hear the fear in my voice if I responded, but I had to respond!

"Yes?" I said as calmly as I could.

"What is the address here?"

I couldn't believe what was happening, he didn't know I was one of the runaway girls? My clothes were torn, my shoes were muddy, and I could only imagine what the rest of me looked like! How could he not know?

I replied, "I am visiting my aunts, and I don't know the address." To my utter surprise and disbelief, one of the women confirmed that I was indeed their niece and they rattled off the address to the gentleman.

I heard him say as he left, "We found one girl at the front of the community with her boyfriend. I guess the other girl has eluded us." He walked out the door and shut it behind him never to be seen again.

I looked up at my saviors with tears rolling down my face, I sobbed uncontrollably, and they were overcome with compassion. Now what? I am sure that is what all three of us were thinking at that time. We all just sat for several moments. "Who can we call for you they asked?"

"I sobbed uncontrollably, and they were overcome with compassion."

"I want my Grandma," I wailed. "Please can I call my Grandma in California?" "Of course, you can!" they said. I dialed information for my dad's mother's number, and as I waited for the phone to connect, I could feel my life being propelled in a brand-new direction.

When I heard the soft crackling voice on the other end of the line say, "Hello?" I lost it!

I told my grandma everything. The truth about him, the truth about my mom, and about how I had escaped.

Within days, I was put on an airplane by these two women who rescued me. They kept me in the safety of their home until then. They fed me, clothed me and kept me hidden until the day they took me to the airport.

As I left, they gently hugged me and placed cash in my pocket. I was never to see them again.

I walked down that ramp to the airplane knowing it was over, and my mother and her boyfriend would never EVER hurt me again!

Your Notes

When was a time in your life you finally felt free? What did you get freedom from: physically, emotionally, mentally or spiritually? Describe the feeling:

_____

_____

_____

_____

_____

_____

_____

_____

_____

_____

_____

_____

_____

_____

_____

_____

_____

Babies
& Wedding Cake

Chapter 9

"Addiction is a disease that makes you too selfish to see the havoc you created or care about the people whose lives you shattered."

I began my new life in California with excitement and anticipation. Everything was going to be ok now! Nothing could ever be worse than where I came from; I was ready for anything, or so I thought.

I went to live with my dad, his longtime girlfriend, and her two daughters. I don't know what I was expecting but this didn't feel right either. I didn't feel like I belonged; I still felt empty and ashamed.

Looking back, I know now that I should have immediately gone into counseling, but that was never discussed or offered. Instead, I was offered marijuana.

"Here," my dad said. "This will help!"

And it did ... for awhile. I felt numb and refreshingly at peace.

Thus, began the slow incipiency of a life of drugs and alcohol. I started attending Helix High School in La Mesa, California in my ninth grade year, I felt so alone. I wanted so badly to be accepted by somebody, anybody.

By now, I was a full-blown cigarette smoker, I started my day off with a cigarette at the taco shop in front of the school. This is where I met a group of people that I fit in with - the "stoner group"! I did not consider myself a stoner, but they were so inviting and welcoming. It wasn't long before I was smoking marijuana every day before school with them. I began ditching classes then completely ditched school. I missed most of my ninth grade year.

"But the rest of the family thought I was a nuisance!"

I was ultimately sent to continuation school and was becoming a heavy burden on my dad's family. I'd hear them fighting about me. Dad felt guilty and wanted to help me, but the rest of the family thought I was out of control and a nuisance.

It wasn't long before I just stopped coming home altogether. I was looking to be loved and began searching for it from bed to bed.

I met my first husband through a friend from school. He was her brother. He was twenty-one, and I was 15! I'd get my weed from him, and it wasn't long before he was providing me with massive quantities of cocaine and alcohol as well.

He lived with his mother, but he had a good job and nice cars, plus all the drugs I could ever want. I could tell he was taking an interest in me, and although I was not interested in him, I still had sex with him.

I felt obligated since he was giving me the drugs I so desperately desired. I justified that I was paying him back, since I had no money. This was a learned behavior. Sex in exchange for having my needs met.

It wasn't long before I found myself pregnant with his baby. Pregnancy had never crossed my mind! When I shared the news with him, to my surprise, he asked me to marry him. I felt I had no other choice; I said yes.

Some family members thought I should consider abortion, but in

"I wanted to prove myself as a good mother."

my mind, it wasn't even an option. I knew I was young, but I felt very old. I wanted this baby; I needed this baby!

I wanted to prove myself as a good mother, loving unconditionally, unlike what I had experienced. I could love without judgment or condemnation. I could love freely and wholeheartedly, because I knew that was what I'd craved. So now, I could lavish love on someone who would never leave me.

I couldn't believe I was going to be a mother and a wife! I'd have my very own house and my very own rules! Now I was in charge; I could run my own life, and no one could tell me what to do. This was my salvation, not only from being alone and unloved, but from being a burden on my Dad and his family.

I wanted so badly to be a good mother, to be everything my own mother wasn't. I vowed I would never ever hit my child or let anyone else lay a hand on them. And we could both eat ice cream out of the tub, 6 inches from the TV!

It was exciting to start this new life. I justified that my husband was a drug dealer, and at times verbally abusive and controlling, but he wasn't a pedophile and didn't hit me. That was enough for me. Those were my thoughts as a 16-year-old girl marrying a 22-year-old man.

"It was exciting to start this new life!"

My baby came two weeks after I turned seventeen. As I lay in the hospital bed holding this little precious angel, a flood of love washed over me like never before.

For the first time, I felt a deep sadness that I didn't have a mother to share this moment with. That emptiness would be felt many more times over the next several decades.

I named my little girl Amanda. The name was significant in that it meant "worthy to be loved."

I was fortunate enough to not have to work. My husband could provide a nice income for us and before long we had purchased our new home. A double wide mobile home in Spring Valley.

My very own home!

I was so excited! It did not matter that the carpet was a green shag and the walls a brown paneling.

To me it was beautiful!

I decorated Amanda's room in Care Bears and rainbow colors. I took great pride in making sure our home was clean and comfortable. I dressed my little one in beautiful dresses and kissed her all the time. I couldn't keep my hands off her! I wondered if my mom had ever taken to me like this when I was a baby.

"Did she ever feel that overwhelming rush of love ...?"

Was I kissed and comforted when I cried, or was I left alone to cry it out? Did she show me off to all her friends and dress me in pretty pink dresses? Did she ever feel that overwhelming rush of love that can only happen between mother and child?

Of course, I cannot remember if those events occurred or not, but I pondered often if she ever loved me like this, if she did how could she have ever let harm come into my life without protecting me? How could she not be angry at the mere thought of someone hurting her child?

Becoming a mother made me even more astonished at her ambivalence to the pain and torture that was put on me every day. How could anyone hurt such an innocent fragile and helpless child?

Although, I did not have an example in my own life of a loving mother the instinct came alive in me the minute she was born. I was there to love and protect her. It was an innate desire to cherish, and an overwhelming, and all-consuming desire to love no matter what!

Two years later, at 19, I had a son and I named him Jason. I loved the name Jason having once had a crush on a boy named Jason in middle school. His name means "Healer" and is so very appropriate because I felt my heart heal a little when he was born.

"His name means 'Healer' … I felt my heart heal a little when he was born."

It was the roughest pregnancy by far, but his arrival brought so much joy!

I couldn't believe I had been blessed with a boy. What a miracle he was to me. I was going to get to raise a son.

And just two short years later, at 21, Cristy was born. She also was named after a best friend in Middle School. I loved her name, mostly I loved saying it. Her name means "cheerful and friendly; follower of Christ".

.

"I loved her name; mostly, I loved saying it."

Oh, how this name fits my Ms. Cris! She is so cheerful all the time, still to this day. She is so very friendly and has mostly good memories growing up.

Seven years later Alexis came into our lives. She was named after a soap opera star. Her name means "helper and defender". It was through my pregnancy with Alexis that I was to be set free from Meth, I will go more in detail about that later in the book.

All four of my children were given nick names and they have stuck thirity-three years later.

Amanda: "Moo Moo" or "Amanda moo".
Jason: "Son shine"; "my son shine".
Cristy: "Sissy"; "our sissy".
Alexis: "Lexi Lee" or "Waddle" … she was very chubby as a baby and waddled when she walked.

I was overwhelmed with nursing and pregnancies. I had been told as long as I was nursing, I could not get pregnant ... LOL ... that's not true.

Throughout, I used marijuana when I could, but being pregnant restrained the huge flood of addiction that was to come. Before my pregnancies, I'd flirted with cocaine and alcohol. I never wanted to drink because that would make me like them.

I never wanted anything to come into my life that would hurt others, especially my children, until I met methamphetamine.

I remember the first time I used Crystal Meth. It was life-changing. I was weak and Crystal Meth seduced me to believing I was instantly transformed into a powerful woman.

"I never wanted to be a scared little girl again ..."

My mind was opened to all sorts of new ideas about who I thought I was and what I could do. I couldn't believe how good it felt, I didn't feel lost or confused, I was energized and happy. Drugs have a way of making you feel invincible, but drugs were robbing me of the life I really wanted and gave me a false sense of identity.

I never wanted to be that scared little girl again, and I thought this drug was my answer. As with all drugs including alcohol, they always work, until they don't!

It wasn't long until I was thinking of using every day, planning my days and weeks around getting loaded. I remember having the very lucid thought, " I had better stop now or I am going to become addicted."

I think I was addicted mentally the very first time I used meth.

"Drugs made me believe I didn't care - but, they lied."

This is a real danger especially for those who have been harmed. The funny thing is that I didn't really want to be high and I didn't know how to be normal except with drugs dulling the every day ache that lived inside my soul, I just wanted to be normal - to feel good!

I didn't want to think about my mother, or him. I didn't want to care!

Drugs made me believe I didn't care; but, it's a lie! It's only as long as the drug lasts, then the demons return. I would do anything to keep those memories away for fear of returning to that pain! When I was high, the past abuse didn't matter anymore. I didn't care that I was in a loveless marriage, that I didn't have a mother, or a family. I cared about nothing else except getting high. I thought it was the only way I could be a mom to my children.

This is the insidious part of the drug.

I always thought I was a better mother when I was high. I thought I was more engaging and more attentive. I had the energy I needed to maintain the home, the enthusiasm I needed to get through hard days, and the focus to sit and color for hours; to bake and sing and play!

I am sure it all sounds wonderful, but there is another side of the drug that inhibited me from being those things all the time. You can only use meth for so long until you crash.

After several days of being awake the body collapses no matter how hard you try to stay awake. This led to several days of me barely moving off of the couch.

The happy gregarious mom would disappear, and she showed up!

This selfish, self-centered addict, who only wanted to sleep, would rise long enough to prepare meals and change the movie on the television. I despised this person in me, as this was the woman, I was trying so hard not to be. But alas drugs are a fleeting fantasy of normalcy, a false fantasy of stability, and place where no true intimacy is taking place.

"I always thought I was a better mother when I was high."

This was my normal as I had no idea who or what I was.

By the time I was twenty-two, I was a full-blown addict. I was done having babies for awhile, and didn't have pregnancies or nursing to restrain my addiction.

I remember many times, sitting on my living room floor after being up for several days crying out to God to save me. My heart would pound so hard in my chest. I just knew I was going to be found dead in the morning. I would beg God not to kill me. I would promise I'd change, only to find myself back on the same floor crying the same prayer every week.

"I wanted a way out of the prison of my addiction, but I was stuck."

I wanted a way out of the prison of my addiction, but I was stuck. I was a high school drop-out with a ninth grade education, no job, no money, and no way to support my children on my own!

I would beg my husband not to bring the drug home, but he knew my weakness and how to keep me under his control. I couldn't stop, and I knew if I did not leave him, I was going to die. He had no desire to quit, but I did.

I couldn't believe this was my life! I had escaped the prison of my youth, only to enter into another one, formed at my own hands. So I did what I knew best. After seven years, I packed my suitcase once more, but this time there were three more bags to pack and three more lives to rescue.

I was not alone any more and my life was not my own, it belonged to these amazing creatures that I vowed to love and protect. I walked out that door at twenty-two, with three babies under the age of five, and what I could fit into my yellow Chrysler Le Baron.

By the time my husband got home from work, we were gone, but he did not let me leave without severe consequences. I was able to get welfare, food stamps and the county helped me rent an apartment. We had no furniture except for a small TV in the living room.

> *"I was not alone anymore, and my life was not my own."*

Family and friends donated beds and basic necessities. I was able to get a side job and save a few extra bucks to buy myself a bed, a water bed! I had always wanted one.

My ex-husband harassed me and terrorized me regularly with threatening phone calls, He would break in and put knives in my walls; and, he slashed my water bed. I had picked up a small job on the side as a limousine driver, and he slashed the tires on the car I drove for work. He slashed my friend's tires, too. Of course, he withheld money, food, and diapers. I kept my resolve I would not go back. I vowed to keep my children fed and safe no matter how bad it got!

"It was an innate desire to cherish; an overwhelming and all-consuming desire to love no matter what."

Your Notes

Who are the people in your life - your kids, relatives? What do they mean to you? What feelings do they spark to life in you? Are you growing into the person they need?

_____

_____

_____

_____

_____

_____

_____

_____

_____

_____

_____

_____

_____

_____

_____

_____

_____

_____

Limousines &
Carlos Murphy's

Chapter 10

*"We only change when we become more committed to
our dreams than to our comfort."*

I was now legally able to get into a bar. Imagine that! Three kids, married for seven years, and I couldn't even legally order a cocktail!

I didn't feel twenty-two; I felt like I was fifty-two.

Bobby McGee's was the local spot where all the girls my age were going, and I was invited by a friend to check it out with her. The invitation meant so much to me ... and I had fun! I never realized how much I loved dancing until I started on these outings.

But with the dancing came drinking, and ultimately multiple sexual encounters. I was there every weekend once again looking for love the only way I knew how to get it.

The attention I was receiving was intoxicating and I craved it. I felt beautiful and desired.

My mother had told me I was ugly on so many occasions that I truly believed I was ugly and if someone paid attention I was lucky. My life was a swinging door of men over the next two years.

I supported my social life by driving limousines at night. It was the only job I could find that required no special talent. My sister watched my children, so I didn't have to pay for childcare.

I met my second husband. He was one of my limousine fares. That night I was not impressed with him. He was drunk and obnoxious. He had no money to pay me for the ride at the end of the night. He was scary and out of control.

"The attention I was receiving was intoxicating - I craved it."

I went to his house the next day to get paid, and thought, "What a loser!"

Several months later, I went to visit my high school girlfriend at her new job at Carlos Murphy's Restaurant. I was shocked to see the same guy walking down the ramp wearing an Assistant Manager shirt!

"Wow", I thought, "he is relatively handsome when he is sober!" He asked me for my phone number and I didn't resist. That night he invited me to a Christmas party and we were inseparable. I ended up moving in with him 4 weeks later, but without my children.

He was 25 and didn't want three kids. I had to make a choice, and the choice I made was in the best interest of myself - the kids went to live with their dad.

I fell into a hopeless pit of despair. I thought I needed him! Without him I was a nothing and a nobody. I had to have his love at any cost.

I chose the love of a man; and, this decision would impact me and my kids for many years.

> *"Being sober was too painful, so I made sure I never was."*

That was all I knew: to choose survival over anything else. Mom chose him over us, and I chose him over them. I moved in, and my addiction went into a full blown tailspin. I lived to get high and got high to live.

I had remorse and pain piled on remorse and pain.

Being sober was too painful, so I made sure I never was.

The supply was unlimited if I went back to my ex-husband for it. My ex-husband taunted me with it. He knew my weakness and strategized against me. He began to call me and hang up repeatedly. Then, I found out that was his signal that he had restocked on dope.

My plight was so bad that all I had to do was think about it and my body would react as if I had already used.

I couldn't say no.

There was always a catch. I had to have sex with him to get it, and he always got what he wanted.

Now I was selling myself to my children's father for drugs; I was a prostitute!

I was ashamed of who I was as a human being and a mother. I felt so hopeless, lost and stuck in my life. I thought I had no choice.

My life was on autopilot and the pilot was Meth.

"My life was on autopilot, and the pilot was Meth."

Your Notes

Have you craved attention in your life? Do you crave attention in your life? What have you been trying to fill this craving with? Have you slipped into a life of addiction, or living on autopilot?

_____

_____

_____

_____

_____

_____

_____

_____

_____

_____

_____

_____

_____

_____

_____

_____

_____

The Beginning
of the End
Chapter 11

*"It's when we come to the end of ourselves that
we come to the beginning of God."*
- Billy Graham

I vividly remember the day the call came in saying my children's grandmother (their dad's mom) had passed away. I felt as if I had been punched in the gut ... my head spun. I had to make a choice; I knew I had to step up! She'd been the safety they needed; she was their sole guardian. By now, 5 years had passed and the kids were mainly living with her. If I didn't do something, they would be with their father full time.

I went to my boyfriend, looked him boldly in the eyes, and said, "I am going to get my kids". I left no room for discussion.

For the first time I stood up for myself, and it felt amazing!!!

For all my life my choices were made for me, for the first time I found the courage to make my own choice.

The very next day, their dad met me in a park with Jason and

Cristy. He held two paper bags filled with some of their personal belongings. Amanda 11 now, Didn't want to come. She wanted to finish out the school year. There were only a few months left and I didn't blame her. I didn't feel I had any right to demand anything from her, so I agreed.

I remember driving back home that day, filled with new hope and inspired to once and for all clean up and become the mother these beautiful humans deserved. I felt invigorated and my chest was warm with love. But was my love enough?

> *"I remember driving back that day, filled with new hope."*

What did I need to do to truly change the trajectory of my life and that of my children?

Summer time came, and my oldest, Amanda, moved in. I wish I could say that having the kids back changed me, but it did not.

Alcohol was becoming a big event in our home and it was more accessible than meth. I was now living 45 miles away from their father and I knew no one else who used it or how to get it.

I would drink then begin to crave the drug. Once the obsession hit me, there was nothing that would get in my way.
It didn't matter how drunk I was or who tried to stop me, I was out of control and hell bent on getting my fix.

One Saturday we had been drinking all day and I had been using meth for a couple of days already. I wanted to get more. Usually I

"I was a train-wreck, and everyone in the way a casualty."

could convince my boyfriend to partake with me but not this time. He was not going to have it. He loved to drink, but he really was beginning to hate meth and everything it brought into our lives: the lies, the disappearing, and the stealing. I did it all. I was a full-blown junkie and did what all good junkies do. I was a train wreck and everyone in my way was a casualty.

This night he tried to stop me!

I remember deciding to start a fight with him. I would get him to hit me or lay his hands on me; then, I would call the police and have him arrested so I could use. Yes that is how sick I had become. The fight was loud and brutal with screaming, yelling and hitting ... but it was me hitting him.

The police were called, and within minutes of arrival an arrest was made; but, it wasn't him - it was me!

I was arrested on domestic violence charges.

How was this happening? I screamed and yelled at the police officers that they had the wrong person!

The Beginning of the End

I was indignant and verbally abusive.

I was booked into Los Colinas Detention Facility in San Diego, California. The date was September 15 1996. I had been up now for three days and by the time I was put into my cell I crashed so hard that I could not be kept awake no matter what.

My body had taken all it could take. I slept for forty-eight hours. When I awoke, I found myself in a nightmare. "Where was I?" ... "How did I get here?"

"My babies!" ... "What have I done!" My children had just come back and now I was gone. My heart ached and so did my body. The emotional pain was more than I thought I could bear. I just wanted to sleep and never wake up. The depression and self-loathing flooded me like a familiar blanket.

"An arrest was made; but, it wasn't him - it was me!"

I hated myself! I just wanted to die!

"It was an innate desire to cherish; an overwhelming and all-consuming desire to love no matter what."

Your Notes

Where was that place you came to the end of yourself only to realize it was the beginning of a deeper relationship with Jesus? Describe your feelings in that moment:

_____
_____
_____
_____
_____
_____
_____
_____
_____
_____
_____
_____
_____
_____
_____
_____
_____

Los Colinas Woman's Detention Facility

Chapter 12

"God goes to the places know one expected they'd ever be so they'd see Him in a way they'd never seen!

When I finally woke up, I looked around the large bunkroom and there were women everywhere. I was in a daze, but slowly began to remember the details leading up to my arrest, and the full realization of what I had become. My tears began to flow. I had spent fourteen years in a drug induced fog.

My body and mind longed to be peacefully numbed by my "once best friend." It gave me the peace I longed for just a little while. But this drug had become the enemy of my life. It wanted me dead. The noise was deafening around me as these women went about the business of the day. My head was still heavy, and my body ached from being asleep for so long.

Each bunk had its own wall, and on each wall, there were pictures and mementos of each woman's life. Some had pictures of their children, their husbands, parents, and friends. Some were so filled up with their outside lives you could barely see the wall. Others were sparse with just a few snapshots into their former lives.

Maybe these women had no one on the outside who cared and sent pictures? What would my wall look like? Would people visit me? Would I have a lot of pictures or just a few? I slowly descended from my bed and headed to the bathroom with the few toiletries I had been given at my booking: a small toothbrush, toothpaste, and a comb.

I made my way to the bathroom and stared into the small mirror above the sink. My eyes had dark circles and my skin was pale yellow. I had barely eaten or had anything to drink in seventy-two hours, and my body felt it. I managed to brush my teeth and run a comb through my hair as I heard the

"I was starving and needed sustenance"

announcement to line up for lunch. It was a welcomed call. I was starving and needed sustenance.

I made my way back to the bunkroom and tried to avoid anyone who looked like they might want to talk. I didn't want to interact with any of these women - they scared me; and, they seemed so resigned to their fate. I couldn't allow this to happen to my life. I had been a prisoner of my own mind all these years ... and now to lose my freedom?

The women chatted with each other, and I listened in. My mind began to whirl with all the stories I heard about women's prisons. My fear began to rise from my belly into my throat. I wanted to cry and run away, but I couldn't let them see I was afraid.

I had to be tough if I was going to make it.

I made it to the lunchroom, and I took the plate that was tossed over to me by a large woman with small black eyes that seemed to pierce right into my flesh. These women think I'm bad. They think I'm one of them, but I'm not! My mind screamed, "I don't belong here!"

"I had to be tough if I was going to make it!"

I thought about my time at Johnny Grey Jones and how I longed to be locked up and protected. This is not what I wanted now. I wanted to be home; I wanted my life back. Just not the life I was living. Something had to change.

I ate my lunch in silence.

After the meal, we were taken into a large room with books and games. There was another lady there, but she wasn't a prisoner. She was dressed in regular clothes and her hair was neatly pinned on top of her head. Her face was kind and gentle. I was immediately drawn to her.

Maybe she reminded me of my grandmother; maybe she gave me a sense of safety. I don't know, but I know I needed her. The books were mostly religious of nature and she saw my inquisitive stare. I walked over to where she stood and looked at the books in her cart.

She asked me my name and we began a conversation. I found out she was the chaplain for the women's prison and came often to minister to the women and bring books. I told her a little about myself. I told her it was my first time being in jail (and I think she could tell).

I feigned interest in her literature as we chatted, but then I came across a book that grabbed my attention. The book was called "The Power of Prayer" by Stormie O'Martin. I can't tell you why it intrigued me, but my hand reached out to grab it. I gently put it on top of my magazines and headed back to my bunk.

I began to chat with some of the ladies that didn't seem so intense. One of those women was a large black lady with a very kind face and motherly demeanor. She seemed to like me, and for some reason, I felt safe with her. I have always been drawn to nurturing women, looking for the mother I never had.

"I felt safe with her; I was looking for the mother I never had."

She looked at me and asked, "Is this your first time in?"

"Yes," I replied.

She looked back at me sheepishly and with great conviction stated, "Yea, well it won't be your last; we ALL come back!"

Those words fell on me like a ton of bricks to my chest. I began to tremble and shake, terrified it could be my fate.

What does that even mean? Don't I have a choice? Is there some force that draws us back no matter what?

In that moment, I felt a shift, and I felt something loud in my body and my throat that wanted to scream the words: "I DO HAVE A CHOICE!" and "I WILL NEVER COME BACK HERE!"

"I do have a choice ... I would find a way to have a choice!"

My entire life had been dictated by someone else's choices - someone else's ideas of what my life would be like. NO MORE! I WOULD find a way to have a choice!

I began reading the book that so intrigued me in the library. At first it seemed mundane and uninteresting, but I continued as if there was something beyond me, pushing me to read it.

Then it happened! I read those words that would change my life in an instant and stay with me forever. The words that put my life on a path that would lead me out; the words that began to set this captive free:

"Praise God for everything in your life no matter what! Be grateful for every situation!"

What? Be grateful for everything?

For being in jail, for the physical abuse, for the sexual abuse?

For having a mother who abandoned me, and a dad that couldn't get clean and eventually died of a heroin overdose? For the drugs, the abusive relationships, for EVERYTHING?

For some reason I believed it. I bowed my head, but not just my head; I also bowed my heart this time - I surrendered! I was at the end of me! The me that kept trying to control, manipulate and run away from life.

I began to thank God for being in that cell with those women, for the police officers who took me away, and for all the circumstances that brought me to this place.

Before long, a peace came over me that I was not used to. I felt a sense of joy and a hope that I had never felt before! I could be here, in this place, and I WILL BE OK!

God was in control of everything not me. All I had to do was praise Him, and from my tiny new space inside the jail cell, that was all I could really do!

Over the next several days I would come to know a few of the women and my newfound lightness and peace had become contagious. Although I was behind bars, I was now freer than I had ever been in my life.

I went to my arraignment fully expecting to serve time. I had several bench warrants and an unsatisfied DUI.

"My newfound lightness & peace had become contagious."

I'll never forget sitting in the holding cell waiting to go in front of the judge singing at the top of my lungs Amazing Grace! There were two other women in with me awaiting their fate as well.

All 3 of us were singing so loudly I am surprised they didn't shut us up, but they didn't. We sang the lyrics over and over until we were led to the courtroom.

It was all a haze, but I remember something being said about reducing the charges from Domestic Violence to a drug charge. I admitted my guilt and returned to my cell at Los Colinas. I was to appear in a few more days for sentencing.

I rode back to the prison in the big green sheriff's bus. Gazing out the windows at the cars driving next to us, I saw people singing along to the radio. I imagined some were pushing down a snack while driving home to be with their families. I was envious of their freedom; they looked so carefree. Again, I longed to be normal ... to have the happy life I had dreamed of for so long.

That evening, I sat up in my bunk going over the events of the day. I prayed " God, your will be done." I picked up my book and began fading into the words until I heard over the loudspeaker, "Catherine, Roll up!"

"I prayed, 'God, your will be done'"

"That's me!", I thought. I looked around at the other women in bewilderment and asked, "What does that mean?"

One of the women grunted back to me, "It means you're going home."

"What?" ... "I'm going home?" ... "Now?"

I jumped from my bunk, ran to the door and waited for the jailer to open it. My mind raced. Does my boyfriend know to come and get me? Do my kids know their mommy was coming home?

I began to cry in gratitude, "Thank you Jesus! Thank you Jesus! Thank you Jesus!"

My charges were reduced to a drug charge, and I was sentenced to a year of chemical dependency classes and AA with time served.

I was released on September 26 , 1996. Did I go back?

Did the incessant call of methamphetamine win out again?

No, It did not!

I never touched that insidious drug again!

One week after coming home, I found out I was pregnant with baby number four ... my Alexis.

I was excited and scared!

I was doing everything I was court ordered to do to stay clean, and now I had even more help. My boyfriend was excited about the baby and so was I. We decided to get married and make it a family

Although our marriage lacked the foundation of trust and any intimacy due to all the trauma over the last 8 years, we did our best to push the past behind us and move forward for this tiny new life growing inside of me.

Life got really, really good. My daughter was born, I began working as a property manager in the community I lived in, and order was starting to appear in my life. I was learning to live life as it came and be ok. When I walked out of my mother's house, I had no idea how to manage my emotions, set boundaries, or ask for my needs to be met. I was starting to feel and act like a real person.

Each day away from drugs set a unique challenge; but, everyday I didn't use I felt stronger. Unfortunately, I did not consider alcohol a drug. It was never a real issue for me so I continued drinking. Bottom line, I am an addict and alcohol is a drug I so quickly found out. I can be addicted to concrete if it altered me from the neck up.

From twenty-nine to thirty-nine, I drank. Sometimes a lot and sometimes a little. Sometimes I blacked out and sometimes I didn't, there

"My life didn't resemble an alcoholic at all"

were days I woke up in my vomit and others I drank like a lady.

My idea of an alcoholic was someone living on a park bench with a brown paper bag in their hand begging for money, my life did not resemble that at all.

I was now living in Temecula California, I was a homeowner a reputable businesswoman, I owned a nice car, I went to church every Sunday and I didn't drink every day.

Boy did I fight this one.

I had battled so hard over the last decade to be free, but here I was loosing again ... this time with booze.

I was coming to a point where I could see I had to make a decision. I heard God's voice daily, "This is not my will for you ... let it go!"

"Please God", I begged, "just let me have this!"

How could I have nothing to numb that pain that still lingered deep in the recesses of my heart and soul?

"Surely you will allow this one thing!!" I bargained and pleaded.

So here I was once more looking down the barrel of a gun. A gun I was holding to my own head!

Would I settle?

Would I let this be good enough?

I had the nagging thought, its only going to get worse! In a moment of clarity I saw the choice: drink or die. Would I give my choice away?

No!

My choice was to walk away and into the rooms of recovery!

Your Notes

When was a time you RESOLVED to change? Where and why did you decide to change? What worked for you after that moment? What didn't?

_____

_____

_____

_____

_____

_____

_____

_____

_____

_____

_____

_____

_____

_____

_____

Reconciliation

Chapter 13

*"A Mother's love and tender care make happiness
grow everywhere!"*

T he restaurant buzzes with excitement! It's filled with families and friends celebrating each other and life. I walk
towards the hostess stand and a cute young girl looks up at me
from behind, her dark curls falling across her forehead and into
her eyes.

"How many in your party?" she asks.

"I have a reservation for fourteen at 5:30 pm," I reply. I'm filled
with gratitude as I think about how blessed I am to have such a
big, amazing family.

The hostess notes that we have arrived, and then we're directed
into the lounge to wait for the rest of the party. I sit down with
my husband and my youngest daughter for the birthday girl to
arrive. My third daughter is turning twenty-nine today! How did

that happen? Where has the time gone!

My "babies" are now thirty-two, thirty, twenty-nine, and twenty-one!

My oldest daughter arrives with my three grandchildren. Next to arrive is my son and his longtime girlfriend. Finally the birthday girl with my granddaughter!

We are directed to our table and settle in for a wonderful evening of connection and celebration. I sit back in wonder at the miracle before me.

What I see is reconciliation and forgiveness at its most beautiful. I often think I don't deserve the life I have today. I took all of this for granted for a long time, and I didn't cherish the gifts I was given.

"I sit back and in wonder at the miracle before me."

Oh, how I wish I could have their childhood to do over, but the past is gone, and all I have is now. I will cherish my now forever, and I'll never take my blessings for granted again.

I live by this statement: "As far as it is humanly possible, be reconciled to everyone!"

"Make every effort to live in peace with everyone and to be holy; without holiness no one will see the Lord."
- Hebrews 12:14

Over the last decade I have made several attempts to reconcile with my mother, because yes, I do believe that we are to make every effort to live in peace.

In this area of my life, I have not experienced a lot of peace. I was always wondering if there was something I could've done different, said something different, acted differently, or been a better daughter.

Once I had a few years of sobriety under my belt there was an opportunity granted to me to extend the hand of peace and reconciliation.

Her mother was sick, and she was coming out to support her and my heart was touched to reach out and extend my condolences.

"There was an opportunity to extend the hand of peace and reconciliation."

I also offered her a place to stay while she was in town. She accepted my offer to stay with me and for a time things seemed to be going well. We did not talk too much about the past as I was in a space of just wanting to let it be.

I didn't feel the need to rehash everything. I wanted it gone, dead, and buried. If there were burdens on her heart I would make it safe for her to share. I guess there weren't because it never came up. I rationalized by saying we are just letting it go.

I was just happy to be with her in a seemingly safe space, me as a grown up now with my own family that I got to share with my mom.

I had longed for this for so long.

She had buried her husband, my abuser, and she seemed to be on a new journey of transformation. While she was here, we had a lot of wonderful talks over our morning coffee and even prayed together.

"I was just happy to be with her."

She got up and read her bible every morning and we chatted about her readings and mostly what was going on in her life. She was in a relationship that was confusing to her and that is where the conversation mostly landed.

As the week progressed and from time to time, I began noticing a slight shift in her temperament from loving and gushing to irritated, judgmental, and gossipy. There was also a lot of self-pity. She didn't have many nice things to say about our family, her sisters, and even my sister with whom I thought she had a great relationship with.

This all confused me, but I didn't know her life well enough to interject, so I just listened and made subtle attempts to change the conversation.

I do not like gossip, nor did I engage; but, I was afraid to oppose her. She is not someone who likes to be challenged. I did glean that over the time we were together.

"I tried not to judge her or create an opinion."

I was as real and transparent as I felt safe being. I tried not to judge her or create an opinion in such a short time. I was kind and gentle ... just allowing things to be.

My grandma got better, and my mother returned home. We continued to chat on the phone, on occasion, and she would even mention the possibility of moving to California now that he was gone.

In 2012, I finally filed for divorce from my husband. Both of us had worked hard to save the marriage, but to no avail. The trauma from my past and from our past together was too much for me to carry. The darkness was creeping in, and I felt hopelessly stuck ... like I had no choice. The revolving theme of my life!

I had started my own business and it had become very successful over the last five years. I could now support myself and my daughter. I had five years sober, and I felt the risk of relapse was far behind me.

I shared my decision with my mother. I had been honest with her, letting her know that my husband and I were having severe problems, and I just didn't know how much longer I could make it.

She took the news well and seemed very supportive.

Once I filed for divorce, everything changed. The old mother that I knew returned. I couldn't understand this sudden shift. It was the same behavior; the shifts from one extreme to another in a matter of moments. You just never knew what you were going to get from her and the old fear and anxiety returned.

"It felt like she only wanted to be part of my life if the picture was pretty."

It felt like she only wanted to be a part of my life if the picture was pretty. She never wanted to be a part of my journey if there was pain or the picture didn't look perfect to the outside world.

"What would people think? You're a Christian! Christians don't get divorced! Your life will be cursed from this moment forward! The Lord will not bless this decision and he will never bring you a good man."

These were the words she tossed out to me so very casually.

Where had the woman who wanted to make things right and talk about the past gone? Did she not realize that I had spent decades undoing the damage that she and her husband had poured into my life?

I had shown her consideration and respect by not rubbing the past in her face. Where was her respect for me as a grown woman making a decision I knew was best for my life?

I watched as the relationship deteriorated right before my eyes and the old feelings of fear, abandonment and loneliness returned.

For my own mental health, I chose to back away and once again close the door to her abusive insane behavior. Once I shut her out, I closed all doors of access and resigned myself that there would be no relationship with her.

"I chose to back away and once again close the door."

In 2014, I was getting married and I wanted so badly for her to be a part of this wonderful new start to my life. I wanted her to see that the decision I had made was good, and that God had blessed it. Maybe, I just wanted to show her that she was wrong.

It was my third marriage and I was finally having a wedding - the wedding I had always dreamed of. I had the pretty dress, the venue, bridesmaids, the food, the music; a real wedding to a man I WANTED TO SAY, "I DO", TOO!

So I took down the barriers and I invited her to my wedding. She said yes. Once again I extended the hand of peace and said, "Let's put the past behind us and move forward."

This time the change happened even faster. All her anger returned and was poured out on me in ways that were so very hurtful. After she returned home from my wedding, I had no choice but to close the doors yet again.

"I have reconciled with many in my life"

"Happy birthday to you, Happy Birthday to you, Happy Birthday dear Cristy, Happy Birthday to you!"

I am brought back to my beautiful life with these words being sung loudly and cheerfully with clashing cymbals. We clap, sing, and cheer on the birthday girl.

My life is glorious and filled with love and connection. I have reconciled with my children and many others in my life. To those I hurt in my disease, I have told I am sorry. Some have accepted it and some haven't. It's unfortunate that there are those who can't forgive. I do understand! I know hurts can be hard to let go of. For those, I just pray and hope someday they can forgive; if not for me, then for themselves.

Unforgiveness is a bitter pill. I know because I dosed on it daily. The only person it ever hurt was me.

Your Notes

How's God work of reconciliation showing up in your life? Are you living in gratitude for healing and restoration? Any relationships that you struggle with?

_____
_____
_____
_____
_____
_____
_____
_____
_____
_____
_____
_____
_____
_____
_____
_____
_____
_____

Competitor
Chapter 14

*"When God has selected you, it doesn't matter who has
rejected or neglected you; God's favor outweighs
all opposition - you are a winner!"*
- Unknown"

As I step out onto the stage my body begins to shake, and
my lips tremble as I try to muster up a smile that says,
"I belong here, I am confident, and I'm a winner!"

My mouth goes completely dry and the smile is now stuck to my
teeth!

Oh my, the sight I must be! Can the audience tell? Do they see me
shaking? I didn't come this far and put in all this work to fall apart
now!

I push down the fear and walk tall. One foot in front of the other,
in 4.5-inch heels and an itsy-bitsy, teeny-weenie, bedazzled bikini.
I'm competing in Muscle Beach's Memorial Day Classic. It's a
beautiful day here in Venice Beach, California, and the crowd is
cheering as the bikini competitors start lining the stage.

I am an athlete. I am a competitor and I have trained for 9 months to take part in this competition. I strike my front pose just like I practiced, and I wait for the other girls to take their turn.

The women are beautiful inside and out. We've all worked so hard, hours and hours in the gym, with many a sacrificed meal and life events. We have a common bond in our fitness achievements, but we all have separate personal goals and motivations for being here.

Winning is not my motivation. Being able to push through my unhealthy relationship with food and my body is my motivation. I've been abusing food my entire life. I exercised to eat!

"Winning is not my motivation."

If I exercised, I could eat; but, if I didn't exercise I would withhold food as a punishment. At my worst, I was binge eating and exercising like I used drugs and alcohol.

From the moment I woke up until I went to bed, I was calculating calories in and calories out. It was exhausting and time consuming. It was just one more area of my life that was out of control and taking away my choices

I was trapped on a hamster wheel, and I could not get off. I needed a solution, but nothing I had done so far had relieved my obsession. I prayed and sought God in this area, I sought advice, and I looked for wise counsel. I remember the first time I became aware of female bodybuilding. I was online one afternoon and saw a former trainer of mine, whom I respected and admired, standing on a stage in high heels, a bikini, and a trophy in her hand!

What had she done to look like that? She looked beautiful before,

"Something else was transforming as well ... my mind!"

but now every muscle in her body was on glorious display. The human form is so amazing, God's creation in His own image. I have always been enthralled by the intricate details of our physical bodies. Wow! I wanted

that and I was bound and determined to know what she did.

I admired and respected this woman and her values. I knew she had a heart for God and others, so I reached out and picked her brain. I didn't think I wanted to do a show, but I did want to be in peak physical condition.

I started her program in September of 2011, and within just a couple of months, I was losing inches, gaining muscle, and feeling less crazy about my food intake. The meal plan was satisfying and healthy. My cravings for sugar began to subside, and my workouts were producing results I could see!

Something else was transforming as well... my mind. I was developing a healthy relationship with my thoughts around food. I could say no to the foods that weren't serving me, and I was exercising to make my body stronger.

I was changing. I felt more powerful and confident.

As the show date approached, my coach began encouraging me to participate in this competition.

I was hesitant. The thought of being on stage and being judged for how I looked petrified me!

I knew this might be a hard idea for some of my Christian friends to accept, but I was not in this to entice or seduce, I wanted to compete! That's who I am at my core, a competitor and very athletic.

"I felt more powerful and confident."

I felt at peace and made the decision to enter the competition. I was nervous and excited, I love doing new things, things that challenge me beyond my comfort zone.

I was eager to share my plans with my mom even though I had experienced such loss in our relationship ... that little girl in me craving her mother's approval still lingered.

My mom had exercised her entire life. She ordered every new gadget off the T.V. and spent at least an hour a day exercising in our home. She places great value on fitness, so I hoped she would be excited for me, too. Maybe we could find some common ground.

I was hurt by her reaction when I told her!

She berated me and said, "Joyce Meyer would never do anything like that. You are causing others to stumble by prancing around in a bathing suit on stage."

"I am a competitor; I am an athlete!" I responded. "This has nothing to do with wanting sexual attention ... body building is a legitimate sport!"

I went on to defend my point, but it quickly became clear that disagreeing with her, or trying to explain my position, was no use. She was right and I was wrong. I truly thought she would be accepting, even if she wasn't in agreement.

"She was right and I was wrong." In my years growing up, I was drawn to competitive sports. This has always been in my nature. I played volleyball in sixth grade, and I was good at it! I made captain of the team, and was poised to play competitively until we moved.

I also twirled baton competitively and was a majorette in the local town parades where I advanced to Team Leader and Banner girl.

It wasn't long before my mother yet again pulled me out of another sport.

I was a pom-pom girl for the local little league team until my mom found out I was wearing makeup to school and she made me drop out. I would play outside for hours making up dance routines, cheer routines and teaching them to anyone who showed interest.

These activities were the only thing I had that made me feel like I fit in with the other kids on my never-ending search for some sort of "normalcy".

I am a natural born athlete who never had a chance to compete. Due to the circumstances of my childhood, I've had to bury my God-given talents and survive.

"Would I allow criticism to stop me"

Now, here I am with an opportunity to fulfill my lifelong dream of being an athlete. There aren't many sports women in their forties can begin competing in. Body-building I naturally fell into.

Would I allow her criticism to stop me?

Would I allow her perspective of what Christian women did and didn't do to take away another opportunity of mine?

This time I had a choice, and I chose to never let her steal another thing away from me, ever again. I chose to compete!

I could no longer live in the shadow of other people's opinions. I wanted to make my own choices, and the only opinion that mattered is God's opinion.

At the age of forty-four I found myself in the best shape of my life, emotionally, physically, and spiritually.

"I could no longer live in the shadow of other people's opinions ..."

After decades of self-abuse and toxic living, I can say I've never felt better. It was exhilarating standing on the stage that day and hearing the cheers from the crowd. I felt so proud of myself.

God did not judge me for taking part in this celebration of life, my life! He did not condemn me for not being more "modest." In fact, just the opposite! He blessed me with a 1st place win!

That's right, I won 1st place in this competition; but, it wasn't just the placing that made me a winner that day. I am a winner because I didn't give up on myself, and because I didn't allow someone else's opinion to become my truth.

Be strong, do not listen to people who want to bring you down to their level. There's a saying that "other people's opinions are none of our business."

Please believe that!

Everyone has an opinion about everything these days, and they are so quick to throw it out there whether asked for or not. That doesn't mean we don't ask for advice, but we don't have to take it if it doesn't line up with who we are.

"The only opinion that matters is God's!"

Be true to yourself and trust that you have more than just your strength inside of you... you have God's strength lifting you higher than you ever thought possible.

I continued to compete and I do very well. I have a shelf lined with trophies reflecting my hard work and dedication, reflecting what God so lovingly says He will do:

Joel 2:25 "I will restore to you the years that were eaten away by the locusts."

l love the sport. I love the camaraderie with the women, and I love continuing to grow in the area of health and wellness. I'm not bound to calorie counting, measuring and yo-yo dieting.

I am very aware of what I eat, but I am no longer in bondage to it. If I want to splurge, I set a day or a meal aside, and I treat myself. I try not to be a hostage to the scale; and, I work hard to keep this area of my life in balance.

My looks and my body can be an idol. I have used it many times to get what I wanted instead of relying on the Lord. I stay very close to the truth in this area. In today's climate of social media and perfection I can easily feel myself slipping into comparison and judgment, so I stay on guard.

"I can easily feel myself slipping into comparison & judgment, so I stay on guard!"

I look back and see how I have spent decades surrendering to other people's ideas of how I should run my life, allowing them to be my god.

> **Proverbs 29:25 "Fear of man will prove to be a snare but whoever trusts in the Lord will be kept safe."**

I have learned to stop comparing. We are all unique. If we keep trying to live our lives by comparison, then we miss who we really are and who others are.

If I'm comparing myself to you, then I am unable to celebrate you!

Today, I live in communion and harmony, not in comparison. I love celebrating my achievements and the achievements of others. Competing gave me back my power. It gave me confidence; and, for the first time, I came to believe I can do anything I set my mind to.

God can use anything He wants to get you where He wants you to be. God used sports to help me get to where I needed to be. I had to find my mental and physical strength to celebrate all I have.

"Other people's opinions are none of our business."

Your Notes

Is there a dream in your heart (something you'd love to pursue) but you stop out of fear of others' opinions? What's God's opinion of you? How does His opinion apply to this situation?

_____
_____
_____
_____
_____
_____
_____
_____
_____
_____
_____
_____
_____
_____
_____
_____

Slow Fade

Chapter 15

**"It's in our weakness where
He is strong!"**

I am going to quit today!" I emphatically say to myself. Yes ...
the struggle continues.

I get out of bed and plan my afternoon around an AA meeting
where I am going to finally go and get transparent and honest with
others.

I have been wanting to quit now for almost a year, but I have not
been able to do so. The drug calls me every morning when I open
my eyes. It has become the first thing I think about when I wake
up and the last thing I think about as I go to sleep.

Here I am on the wrong side of addiction, yet again!

Once more I have no choice, I must get high no matter what! I
have fallen victim to the legalization of marijuana. I can't do anything without it.

I can barely stay sober at work counting down the time until my last job of the day is completed. Even at work I am doing only what I must and nothing more. I have become trapped in a prison I created and a prison that I have the key to. The ironic thing is that all day I plan this trip to prison and as soon as the cell slams shut, I am planning how to get out and never come back again.

Insanity - doing the same thing over and over expecting a different result.

I have more anxiety and stress than I have had in a decade.

I am constantly in fear and hiding; I feel emotionally and spiritually dead. My life is completely out of control and I am stuck, again. I have no choice.

"How did I get back here?"

"How did I get back here?" My life is good. I had no reason to want to run away!

I never thought it would happen. I thought I could control it!

It's June 2015 and I am meeting Adam's entire family for the first time. It is his sister's 50th and mother's 70th birthday celebration.

We have all rented homes in Mission Beach to celebrate for several days. I am so excited as I love this man and he loves me. We have been dating for a year now and are both confident that marriage is in our very near future.

In fact, I think he might be proposing this weekend. I can't be sure, but it's in the back of my mind; and, I am giddy with excitement. Everyone is celebrating, and revelry is in the air! Adam's family have come from all over to join in on the festive event!

I am happy and have no desire to drink, but thoughts of using marijuana had begun creeping into my mind since it was legalized.

"Or, did it start with little compromises - no real accountability?"

I don't know how it started, if it started back in the rooms of AA when I would announce quite emphatically to my friends, "If I ever get cancer, I will start smoking pot!" Or if it started with little compromises, less meetings, no sponsor, no real accountability.

Weed isn't a drug. I convinced myself it was medicine, it was legal now in Colorado and California, and with a doctor's prescription you could have it delivered to your front door. Either way I was now at a turning point and ultimately, I chose to get high that weekend.

I rationalized it and justified it to the point it seemed like no big deal. I had quit in 1999 with absolutely no problem, so if it became an issue, I would just lay it down again. I wish I could say I hated it, but alas, I did not.

I was fully expecting that if it was a bad thing in my life I would begin wanting to drink immediately and my life would crash down around me in days. That did not happen.

Adam is a "normie." That's what we call people who drink without the compulsion for more. He doesn't understand the nature of my disease so convincing him was easy. I called my sponsor and one other person in the program and told them that I had decided to get a prescription for medical marijuana under the guise of menopause.

"The one person I didn't consult on an intimate and genuine level was God"

I even went to an AA meeting and disclosed it there. Granted it was a meeting I had never been to, and I never once went back to. The one person I did not consult on an intimate and genuine level was God.

After arriving home from the birthday celebrations, I made an appointment to see a cannabis doctor and plead my case as to why this would be so good for my life. Finding a doctor in my Bible-belt town was easier than I thought. There was one just minutes from my home.

I made my appointment for the same week.

As I drove into the strip mall where the office was located, I noticed a small amount of anxiety begin to creep up. Wow, that was new, I haven't had anxiety in a long time. I chalked it up to being nervous about the appointment.

I was very concerned that with my addiction history the doctor was not going to give me a prescription.

I parked my car and found the door with the green medical sticker. Wow, I thought to myself, this is crazy. Nothing like the 1980's and 90's where I was meeting people in dark parking lots to score my dope. I felt less like I was doing something wrong.

> *"I felt less like I was doing something wrong."*

I pushed open the door and walked inside. The room was large, there were three or four people in the waiting room. A woman came out of the office and asked me to sign in. She seemed nice and did not look like a junkie or criminal. This was getting better and better by the minute.

I was called back into her office where she took my vitals, had me fill out a few forms, and took my $80.00 for the office visit.

I handed it over gladly, seemed quite cheap to be able to smoke pot legally! I was told to wait in the waiting room until the doctor called me back.

I took great notice of the people coming in and out of the doctor's office. They were average looking men and women with ages ranging from 20's to their 70's. Grandmas, grandpas, mothers and fathers. I am not sure what I was expecting to see, but I became more comfortable as the moments ticked by.

My name was called, and I walked sheepishly into the doctor's office fully expecting to be turned away once he found out I was a recovering alcoholic/addict. The form I filled out had not asked, but I was certain it would come up.

"I walked sheepishly into the doctor's office."

As I walked into the room, I saw a large mahogany desk. The room smelled of dust and a slight hint of mildew. I looked around for someone, but there was no one there. I was directed over to a chair facing the desk where a large computer sat.

I eased myself into the chair and immediately saw an older gentleman on the computer screen.

Oh goodness, I thought, this is different!

"How are you Mrs. Schiffer?" he asked.

"I am well, thank you!"

"What brings you out to see me today?"

"Well, I'm hoping to get a prescription for cannabis." This word seemed much more official than pot!

"What are you wanting to use this medication for?" he asked.

"I am moving into menopause, and hoping it can help."

"What are your symptoms, dear?"

"I am not sleeping well, I'm newly married and in love, but still finding myself agitated and depressed. I take anti-anxiety meds and depression meds and they just don't relieve all my symptoms. If this works, I am hoping to begin eliminating pharmaceuticals out of my life and going in a more natural direction."

"Well that I certainly agree with", he replied.

"Dear, I believe medical marijuana will be a great support to you. I have seen many women get the relief they were seeking from cannabis. You can get your card from my nurse on your way out."

That's it?

He didn't even ask about my predisposition to addiction, don't ask don't tell! I can legally use marijuana and if I use the prescription as directed, I would not lose my time in AA, I was ecstatic!

I will not let it get out of control I promised. I was giddy with excitement!

Psalms 81;12 "So I gave them over to their stubborn hearts to follow their own devices."

The unfortunate thing about this prescription is that the directions were "as needed." This was an open end for disaster and I could see that logically, but now my heart was getting harder and I was justifying it more often.

After the first year I could tell things were beginning to change. My anxiety had kicked up to the point I had developed neuropathy in my back. I was having palpitations more often and my fear level was rising. I was noticing insecurity and doubt start to take a hold on my life.

"I couldn't discern God's voice anymore."

I couldn't discern God's voice anymore.

I began to isolate and started to doubt my husband's love for me.

I was not being honest with people about how much and how often I was using. I was back in hiding.

Many times, I swore I was going to quit but, I could not go one day without it. Before I would get high, my mind made it seem so innocent. But after I got high, I would fall under condemnation and guilt. The drug had not only stopped working, but now it had turned on me.

"The drug had not only stopped working, but now it had turned on me."

My Quit Date

"Sometimes you can only find heaven by backing away from the hell!" - Carrie Fisher

I set my first quit date.

As I am driving to my AA meeting the doubt creeps in, maybe I just needed a different strain. Maybe I just need to ingest in a different way.

All these different scenarios begin to circle in my head.

I arrived at the meeting early and sat in my car searching different strains on the internet. I put into the search bar "happiness, relaxation, and clarity."

Several options pop up that promise to deliver these desired effects.

I go into my meeting hoping for a miracle word in that room - something that will make me not want to get high anymore; but, I say nothing. The meeting is over and the one friend that I had been truthful with in the beginning approaches me. I had been honest with him about 6 months earlier that the cannabis was becoming an issue.

"Hey stranger, how are you?" he asked.

"I am good, how are you?"

"I am good too!"

"How are you doing with the cannabis? Are you ready to quit?"

"I am getting closer", I respond.

We part, and I head straight to the dispensary. I pick up my new strain with its promises of peace. I drive home and anxiously dart into my backyard where I proceed to grind up my medicine and load my pipe. I

"I am broken, defeated, hopeless and out of choice in my life"

take a hit and wait for peace to come but that was not to be.

Within minutes I am face down on my living room floor sobbing! I am broken, defeated, hopeless, and out of choice in my life.

A substance is running my life again.

I cry out to God, "Where are you? Why aren't you helping me? Please God make me normal. Make me like everyone else; I just want to fit in. Please don't take this away from me; let me have something!" I plead. "I am so angry at you God! Why can't you just give me this?"

Suddenly, I hear a gentle whisper. "Baby, you can have the cannabis, and your spot in heaven is secure! You will spend eternity with me! But, let me be very clear with you. Do you see where you are right now?"

"Yes Lord, I do!"

"I will give you the strength you need"

"This is as good as it is going to get for you, from here moving forward." ... "Are you willing to settle for anything less than the promised land?"

"Oh God, no", I cry! "I want more", I cry out in despair! Tears are gushing down my face as I continue to ask for relief!

Once again, I hear His voice, "Then lay it down, sweetie; go dump it out!"

"Oh God, no! I don't have the strength to dump it out!" I cried.

"I will give you the strength you need!" He replied.

I walked into my backyard, I picked up my flower pot filled with different strains that promised me all sorts of wonderful things. I grasped it tightly holding it close to my chest. I walked into my bathroom and began sobbing hysterically as the tears pour into the container drenching the contents inside.

"God, I do not have the strength to pour it out, I will give it to somebody."

A booming voice comes back at me, "No one needs it; throw it out!"

"God, I am so weak. I can't just throw it away." I sit and I hear nothing through my sobbing for what seems like an eternity, and then I am gently shaken with a vision.

It's a vision of me sharing with people who are hurting and addicted.

"Yes God, that is what I want, you know my heart is to help the broken hearted!"

"Then throw it away sweetie!"

I walk into my backyard, I pour every little container out into the dirt, still crying all the while.

I pack up all my paraphernalia and He instructs me to drive to Stater Brothers and put it in their trash can as the temptation will be too great if I put it in mine.

I numbingly and grudgingly do as I am told.

"He told me nothing would ever change his love for me"

I drive a mile away, behind the grocery store, to their large industrial trash receptacles and toss it over the wall into the can. It's gone and I feel empty.

I called Adam and through my tears shared with him that I was addicted to marijuana and I can never get high again.

He comforted me, told me he supported any decision I made and that nothing would ever change his love for me.

I climbed into bed and cried myself to sleep.

Dry Bones Come Alive

Quitting this time was not as easy as it had been in the past. Marijuana today is 80-100% THC unlike the 90's where it was 3-5% THC

Sleep eluded me for weeks, I was getting less than 5 hours of un-interrupted sleep a night. I could not eat and began losing weight rapidly. I experienced cold sweats and could not get my body temperature regulated. I was detoxing horribly.

People say Marijuana is not addictive. I am here to tell you it is. I asked God to make it easier and He said, "If I made it easy, it would only make it easier for you to go back." I believed Him.

I craved it daily but leaned on Him moment by moment for strength.

I got honest and transparent with myself and others. I went back to my recovery meetings and shared my experience with marijuana.

There is such comfort and strength in those rooms. In all my years of searching to fit in and belong, this is one of the few places I feel 100% like I fit in. No one understands me like

"No one understands me like another addicted person."

another addicted person. Be it food, alcohol, drugs, etc. we just get each other.

I am experiencing the peace, happiness, and relaxation I was looking for in the weed, and my neuropathy and panic attacks have subsided .

I am sleeping soundly and best of all I am back in my Father's house communing with Him on such a sweet and precious level. And guess what?

Two weeks past the vision I received from the Lord, I was sitting in front of six hurting and struggling women sharing my experience of addiction and redemption. And within months I was granted permission to minister at a women's prison where God is using my story to support incarcerated women.

I haven't done any of this perfectly, and if I said I didn't slip up a time or two, I'd be lying. But, I press on, and I don't quit! It's progress I seek today, NOT perfection! And I thank God for peeling me like a stack of Band-Aids - one at a time! Not the whole darn stack at once - ouch!

He is faithful to his promises and His word never returns void.

1 Thessalonians 5:24 "The one who calls you is faithful; He will surely do it!"

Your Notes

What are the small compromises in your situation? The things that slowly blur your spirit's discernment of God's voice? What practical steps can you take to set healthy boundaries here?

_____

_____

_____

_____

_____

_____

_____

_____

_____

_____

_____

_____

_____

_____

_____

_____

_____

Lot & His Daughters
Chapter 16

"Spiritual abuse can be hard to identify but is no less difficult to endure than any other kind of abuse."
- Unknown

Music Playing! "Every blessing You pour out, I'll turn back to praise. When the darkness closes in, Lord, still I will say, 'Blessed be the name of the Lord; blessed be Your name'"

It is a beautiful Sunday morning and the 9:30 service at church is just beginning our time of worship. The music rocks and we all worship collectively.

I look up next to me at the beautiful man that God brought into my life. I am filled with such awe and wonder as to what God has done for me.

The darkness has closed in so many times, and in the end, it was Jesus Christ who saved me. I have had more blessings in my life than I can count, and it is Jesus Christ who gives them to me.

I am learning to love God through trusting Him, and my faith in

Him has been built through the pain.

When I was growing up, God was talked about daily, but not in a healthy way that drew me near to Him. It was in a way that would send me to the floor on my little knees … shaking.

I was told that the beatings were of God, as the Bible encouraged parents to beat their children: "spare the rod and spoil the child."

I was told over and over that God was coming back some day, and that I would not be able to grab onto my mother's apron strings to get there. My salvation was my problem, and I better get it figured out … I was only 8!

"When I was growing up, God was talked about daily, but not in a healthy way."

We were forced to memorize bible verses and entire chapters with the threat of punishment if we didn't get it right. As I got older, I began to resent this God who I was reading about. Beyond my mom's threats of not going to heaven because I was bad was my step dad's use of the Bible.

He condoned his rapes by telling us that it was okay by God that these things happen. He specifically used the story in the Bible about Lot and his daughters. He told us that Lot had sexual relations with his daughters, and this was favorable to God. He got up every day and read from the Bible for hours, and it was repeated that he had been a deacon in his church, a very prominent man of God. It just made me resent God more and more. What kind of God lets these kinds of things go on?

What kind of God condones beatings and rapes, torture and emotional berating? Not the kind of God I wanted anything to do with. My young life was filled with such confusion about Him that the easiest thing for me was to run away from this mean God who wanted to send me to hell and was looking for reasons to punish me. My young life was filled with such confusion about Him that I did what I knew best - I ran away from him!

I would run in and out of relationship with Him for decades. I ran to Him if I felt like the rapture was imminent or if I found myself in trouble; but, when things were good, He was not even a thought. It wasn't until I went into recovery that I began to dig into the mysteries of who this Being is.

As I began uncovering the truth about God I was in such shock and dismay at how He had been represented to me as a child. They had lied to me about everything. I was never introduced to Jesus. I was held to the law, the rules, and the regulations. Grace was never mentioned.

> **Matthew 18:6 "But whoever causes one of these little ones who believe in me to sin, it would be better for him to have a great millstone fastened around his neck and to be drowned in the depth of the sea."**

When I read the true story of Lot and his daughters, I was enraged. I realized my mother and stepfather changed God's word to suit their illicit behaviors.

Deuteronomy 4:2 "You shall not add to the word I am commanding you nor take away from it."

God isn't a God of anger and punishment. **He is a God of love and second chances.** He is a God of mercy and grace who sent His son to die in my place for my sins past, present, and future.

I don't have to be perfect or rely on my own strength to get to heaven. All I must do is believe! No one ever told me that in my home. I learned that in Sunday school, but everything I learned there was negated by the spiritual abuse going on in my home.

Today at fifty-one, I have a much better understanding of who God is and WHO HE IS NOT!

He is not an angry God looking to jump on you the minute you mess up. He is a loving Father who wants the best for his children. I am clearly not perfect, but God has still shown Himself faithful to me. His strong arm of safety has been around me my entire life. He delivered me from meth while I was still drinking and smoking cigarettes. He delivered me from alcohol and cigarettes during unforgiveness and uncontrollable lust. He brought me an amazing husband even though I divorced. He has given me a healthy body and a strong mind despite all the abuse I put on it! He has blessed me financially even though I have not always been a good steward of His gifts.

> **Romans 5:8 "But God shows His love for us in that while we were still sinners, Christ died for us."**

He loves me like a good parent would, but that was the disconnect. I have never had good parents that reflected the love of Christ. It has been very hard to learn this over the years, and even harder to trust Him.

"His Joy is everlasting"

If you were brought up in a home or church that set your heart against God, maybe you were introduced to the wrong God as well.

We all have a God-shaped hole inside of us and we try filling it with things that do not belong there: food, drugs, men, material things, work, etc. This was all fleeting and did not bring the joy I sought, but His joy is everlasting.

My friend, start looking outside of what you were taught. Ask God to show Himself to you, and He will!

> **Jeremiah 29:13 "You will seek me and find me when you search for me with all your heart."**

Your Notes

What did you learn about God growing up? Did anyone around you use Him to their advantage/agenda? Are you currently searching for Him with ALL of your heart?

_____

_____

_____

_____

_____

_____

_____

_____

_____

_____

_____

_____

_____

_____

_____

Is It Mental Illness?
Chapter 17

"Forgiving - the act of remembering without pain."

O ver the last couple decades people have asked me to consider the possibility that my mother is mentally ill. There was absolutely no way I would agree to that conclusion!

To me, the label "mentally ill" meant you have a get-out-of-jail-free card. Every criminal wants a mentally-insane judgment!

In my mind, my mother rose up every day grabbed a piece of paper and a pen, and looked for ways to infiltrate my life and create pain. She stalked my Facebook account, leaving hurtful messages on my posts. She bombarded my friends, children, and family with messages about how innocent she is and what a liar I am!

She said she would never allow her child to be raped or tortured. That she was a good mother, and had no idea why I had such a vendetta against her.

This did not seem insane to me, this seemed malicious and purposely thought out. She was there. She witnessed the crimes against my body and soul. BY GOD, SHE PARTOOK IN THEM!

I have known her now for fifty-one years, and in my mind, it was all personal and it felt like pure hatred.

So no, I would not consider that she was mentally insane!

And then ... I read a book by Priscilla Shirer called *Fervent*, and in it, she talks about offering forgiveness. Not only offering forgiveness, but COMPASSION as well!

"All you need is a willing heart!"

I have to say when I first read this I was completely taken aback. "Lord, surely this doesn't mean that I am to feel compassion for her?"

And in my spirit, He responded, "Yes!"

How can I have compassion for someone like this? How can I have compassion for someone who sets out daily to make my life a living hell and turn everyone I love against me?

This is not possible!

"You're right my child. It is not possible for you, but for me all things are possible in a willing heart!" He said.

"A willing heart? You mean all I have to be is willing to offer compassion?"

"Yes, just become willing," I heard in a still, small voice.

So I prayed for God to help me become willing. To me, it felt right to hold her accountable for all the pain she has caused me and my family.

It wasn't long that, yet again, someone else offered the suggestion that there was a possibility of mental illness.

Not again, really?! But I contemplated it, and I prayed that if this were the case that the truth would be revealed.

"The truth will set you free." My daily devotion the next morning was: "You will know the truth, and the truth will set you free!" That very afternoon, there was a third suggestion of mental illness. Then, the next day I was in the gym praying and meditating on these words. In an instant, I not only heard it, I received it! I allowed the fullness of that realization to wash over me. She's mentally ill!!

OF COURSE SHE IS!

I was immediately reminded of all the times her eyes were so black and dead; all the irrational behaviors that were so volatile. The changing mood swings that were like a pendulum. The narcissistic behaviors; the all-about-me attitude. The inability to treat a child with love and kindness, and her allowance of such terrible things to happen. It all reeks of mental illness.

It all made sense now!

And in that moment with the acceptance of the fact that my mother had a mental illness, I was able to feel compassion. I felt a deep sadness for her! I felt sad for all the lost years trying to gain her acceptance when clearly that was beyond my control; for all the years I held onto anger and bitterness, and numbed out to survive.

> *"And in that moment ... I was able to feel compassion"*

In the very next moment, I felt extreme gratitude that this was not my story.

I am just an addict, LOL! Whether that be genetic or as a result of the abuse. With that diagnosis there is a solution and hope for a life commited to recovery.

Mental illness is a part of my extended family, I have known that to be true.

Now I have to say, that never has she been clinically diagnosed with a mental illness to my knowledge, so yes, this is speculation. Although she did share with me on one occasion that her therapist has told her she was incapable of telling the truth. Even those words ring mental illness because her reality is her truth, and the

"I am free to let her go"

mind of a mentally ill person creates their own version of truth. Whether that be to protect themselves from pain in their own lives and past, or the inability to cope with reality. I'm not a doctor; I don't know why. But praise Jesus, I don't have to continue to seek answers in this area. I am free to let her go, pray for her and move on with my life!

So with that, what do I do now?

I will continue to prepare my heart and my emotional well-being to be able to receive her if she ever seeks treatment and reaches out from a place of healing. Only God knows the future. It's my job to prepare for all possibilities and put off malice and anger. But there is more!

Not only have I come to a place of compassion for her, But I've also worked really hard to come to a place where I can be somewhat grateful for the things that she taught me.

What could I have possibly learned?

Well, the first thing I learned was what kind of mother and grand-mother I did NOT want to be, LOL!

I am a good cook and she is a good cook. I love exercise and she loves exercise. I love to keep my home tidy and she is a very tidy person. I appreciate nice things and so does she. She is a hard worker and I am a hard worker. The list grows as God shows me new ways to be appreciative instead of being resentful and bitter.

God uses our hardest relationships to teach us something about ourselves.

We can use these difficult relationships to take a more accurate accounting as to who we are by the way we respond to difficult people. We can see where we need to make correction in our own lives, difficult relationships are like sandpaper rub-

"Diamonds are refined in the fire!"

bing off the rough edges and revealing a newer, shinier version of ourselves.

Pressure creates diamonds; fire refines gold!

So, you see, even from the most painful experiences we have in life, we can be grateful for the things they teach us.

I know it's hard. There is so much pain in the life of a child who is raised by a mentally ill person, but we do not have to suffer.

There is hope!

I thought granting her a mental illness plea would be a get out of jail free card for her! But you know what my friends? It has been a get out of jail free card for me!

> **Isaiah 48:10 "Behold, I have refined you, but not as silver is refined; rather, I have refined you in the furnace of suffering."**

Your Notes

Think back on a moment of accepting the truth about a situation or relationship? Did you find freedom in this moment? How did you feel? Did you find the willingness to forgive?

_____

_____

_____

_____

_____

_____

_____

_____

_____

_____

_____

_____

_____

_____

_____

_____

_____

_____

Now What?

Chapter 18

"The past is gone and can't be re-written; but the present is here, and you hold the pen!"

T his is what I want you to take away from this book. This is my heart!

This book was not written to tattle on anybody, rehash the past, or to create pain in anyone's life. This book is my life and exactly the way I remember it.

My purpose in these pages is that we will find hope, freedom, and meaning in the pain ... whatever that might be. Maybe you have a similar story and that's what brought you to this book.

I want you to know that there's nothing special about me, that these challenges aren't unique to me, and that I'm no different than anyone else. I want you to believe the freedom I have found is the same freedom offered to you. I know from my work with other victims that there are countless stories like mine and they too rose above it and became strong vibrant women.

I don't want ANYBODY living with the nagging pain, anxiety, and fear. With the anger that bubbles in our belly and hurts our body, our mind and soul - the anger that I have experienced for so many years. I don't want you living in defeated relationships never knowing true love or freedom.

I want you to know that there is a God who loves you. I want you to know that God didn't put this pain on you.

It was not His will that I was abused. My parents made these choices ... human choices. God has given us all free will, and we live in a fallen world ... a world with very sick people who use their free will to fracture the lives of others, intentionally or otherwise.

"He is behind the scenes working all things out."

God hears our cries, He witnesses our sufferings, and He cries right along with us. I believe God was screaming at them to stop, but they chose not to listen.

He will rescue us if we call on Him and trust that He is behind the scenes working all things out for those that love him.

Romans 8:28 "He works all things out for those that trust in Him."

It might not be as fast as we want, but the healing will come.

**Psalm 147:3 "He heals the brokenhearted
and binds up their wounds."**

I chose drugs and alcohol to bind up my wounds for a very long time. This was the only option I thought I had. I watched them medicate and so did I.

I chose decades of anger, thinking it was hurting her, but it was only hurting me. So, what is the solution, what is the other way?

Well, as cliché as it may sound I learned I need to start talking about the abuse to someone who can support me and help me break free of the trauma. I had to admit the pain was there and stop pushing it down pretending it didn't exist.

"I learned I needed to start talking to someone."

As a victim in this kind of abuse and cycle of addiction, brain grooves are created that last a lifetime. It's easy to fall back into our old way of thinking along with the negative behaviors and degrading self-talk.

Therapy can help change the tapes. I started therapy when I was thirty-three, but it only did a little good until I quit drinking.

I know it is hard to lay down the anesthesia, but if you're anything like me, it's a vital step. Anesthesia is designed to keep you asleep and numbed out. You might feel awake but your feelings are asleep. You have to dig down and get to those feelings. The dictionary describes anesthesia as insensitivity to pain, especially if artificially induced by drugs.

The pain came from a childhood of abuse, but the numbing effect it had on my emotions stunted me and held me back. It prolonged the inevitable AND prolonged the pain. I had to learn how to feel again!

"I had to learn how to feel again."

I learned that I had to be willing to go through just a little more discomfort, but I promise you, it was nothing like what I had endured as a child.

Christ is my Higher Power, my Strength when I have none and my Protection through all of the trauma.

The church organization, Celebrate Recovery, gives me permission to be specific about my God, but if you're in another space with God, then the other meetings like AA might support you better. Maybe your drug of choice is food, sex, or relationship addiction ... there are programs for all of that. I have sat through many of them.

I have a compulsive personality, and I can become cross addicted if I am not on top of my spiritual condition. We can easily be addicted to multiple things. The steps I took are biblically based, and God is in them.

On this journey I have been delivered from many compulsions, bad habits, shame and self-loathing. These are the biblical principals I live by today as I continue to walk the journey of recovery.

Mathew 5:6 "Happy are the pure in heart."

I needed to make amends to the people who had been hurt in my life. Saying you're sorry is not only in words, but also by how you live. Your words mean nothing if you continue hurting people.

Our lives should not look anything like they did. We repent, turn from the past, and start down a new path. If we fall off the path we get right back up and keep on going. This is called an amends we live out daily, and it keeps our side of the street clean at all times.

Mathew 5:7 and 9 "Happy are the merciful, and happy are the peacemakers."

I offered forgiveness to those who have hurt me. What I have learned is that forgiveness does not equal relationship. I can forgive that person but I do not have to be in his/her life.

One way I have been able to forgive is by praying for that person.

Romans 12:14 "Bless those who persecute you. Don't curse them, pray that God will bless them."

I know this sounds very difficult, but we don't have to mean it when we start. We can do it through clenched teeth, but I promise if you keep at it, the softening will come, and feeling of anger and bitterness start to lift.

Romans 12:18-19 "Do all that you can to live in peace with everyone; never take revenge. I will take revenge says the Lord"

These verses encourage me that I don't have to take revenge because He will. Their relationship with God is none of my business.

My life today has everything in it that I have been searching for. Peace, safety, love, true friendships, a healthy marriage and sex life. I am not getting any of it out of a bottle, or a bag, or a person, but I get it all from God. God is the source of the power that's in me today.

"God is the source of the powers that's in me, today!"

The woman I am is strong and powerful. I am no longer a victim or a victimizer.

I walk in victory over the powers of darkness that threatened to kill me for so many years; and I found this victory by bending my knee to the God of the universe and laying all the pain at His feet. I have picked things back up 10,000 times only to find myself back at the cross!

I beg you to give him a chance. He is there waiting with arms wide open and a willingness to wipe all your sorrow and pain away.

"He will take the mess and turn it into a message!"

Not only will He wipe away all the sorrow and restore all the beauty, He will begin doing work through us. He will take the mess and turn it into a message.

God says we are to be His hands and feet to a world of broken people. From the mess my non-profit was born, **One Voice One Mission.** We are a community committed to reducing child abuse and bringing safe-touch curriculum to our schools nationwide.

I have created a platform from the pain. I am being used by God in a mighty way to expose the devil for the liar that he is.

The devil promises us pleasure if we follow him. He studies us and strategizes against us to exploit our weakness, then he comes at just the right moment. When we are at our weakest and most vulnerable, he attacks.

Satan particularly wants to infiltrate the lives of children. If he can turn the heart of a child, he has a good chance of keeping us stuck in a lifetime of defeat.

One in 5 girls, and one in 7 boys are abused by someone they know. Child abuse runs rampant in this world. You see it daily in our headlines, in newspapers, on TV and Social Media.

Children abducted, trafficked, raped, held hostage for decades in houses of torment and pain, and tragically some murdered. The prison systems are filled with adults who were abused physically and sexually as children. It is an epidemic and it has been tearing away at the fabric of our families for decades.

"What if the purpose of our life is being shaped by our greatest pain?"

Today, I am a successful business owner, athlete, speaker, author and life coach. But most of all, I have love, trust and companionship - I have found where I belong!

No more running away; no more hiding from the monsters in the closet! Do I get scared? YES I DO! I'm scared right now as I put pen to paper writing this book! That's where courage comes in ... doing it anyways - in the face of fear!

Acts 27:25 "So take heart, for I have faith in God that it will be exactly as I have been told."

Being in a position of leadership in my church, I hear it asked often, "How I will know God's purpose for my life?" Isn't that what we all seek? Our purpose; why we were born?

Well, what if the purpose of our life is being shaped by our greatest pain, our failures, our biggest hurts and sources of grief?!

What if ALL THE LITTLE PIECES OF YOU are being shaped by YOUR sufferings to lead you to YOUR PURPOSE?!

DON'T BE A VICTIM BE A VICTOR!

Romans 8:37 "No, in all these things we are more than conquerors through him who loved us."

"What if all the little pieces of you are being shaped by your sufferings to lead you to your purpose?"

Your Notes

What has pained you the deepest in life? Do you see a need in our world for your message? What do you hear God saying? Have you asked him to be your Source of Power?

_____
_____
_____
_____
_____
_____
_____
_____
_____
_____
_____
_____
_____
_____
_____
_____

"Forgiveness is not a get out of jail free card for them; it's a get out of jail free card for us!"

about

Since the age of 12 Catherine's had a book on her heart. It has lived there growing and changing over the last 40 years. She has walked through countless obstacles, getting stuck in some of them for many years. Through her teens and into her 30's she battled drug abuse alcohol abuse and 2 failed marriages and many dysfunctional relationships in-between. She raised 4 kids along this journey - kids that had to grow up really fast! As she approached her 40's, something shifted and she knew it was time to change or die. She surrendered her life to Jesus, and that's when her life took on an entirely new and profound meaning! She walked through the doors of recovery and began the daunting journey of undoing all the wreckage in her life -

connect with catherine

Catherine would love to connect with you @ catherineschiffer. com where you can also book her to speak.

some caused by others and some at her very own hands. Now at 51, she can say she is free! Free of substance abuse, bitterness and free to love herself and others. Catherine competes and has won multiple awards as a body builder, is an active realtor and business owner. She's committed to her continued recovery through Alcoholics Anonymous and Celebrate Recovery, and she owns a non-profit whose mission is bringing awareness to childhood sexual abuse. When she's not speaking, coaching, listing a house or working out, she's spending time with her best friend and husband, Adam, or one of her 6 kids or 7 grandkids!

"Turn your mess into a message!"

CPSIA information can be obtained
at www.ICGtesting.com
Printed in the USA
FSHW021419121020